COPPER NICKEL

number 25 / fall 2017

EDITOR/MANAGING EDITOR
Wayne Miller

EDITORS: POETRY
Brian Barker
Nicky Beer

EDITOR: FICTION & NONFICTION
Joanna Luloff

EDITOR: FICTION
Teague Bohlen

SENIOR EDITORS
Alison Auger
Karl Chwe
Steven Dawson
Jennifer Loyd
Vin Nagle
Elsa Peterson
Lyn Poats
Kyra Scrimgeour
Carley Tacker

ASSOCIATE EDITORS
Carolyn Jelley
Zane Johnson
Elise Lakey
Steph Rowden
Tristian Thanh
Grace Wagner

ASSISTANT EDITORS
Caroline Eppers
Aaron Fennimore
Kelsey Foster
Lauren Gombas
Jack Gialanella
Chiahci Lee
Kara Klein
Veronica Mata
Taylor Murphy
Paige Perich

Amber Sullivan
Casey Temple
Chris Traister
Steven Vigil-Roach
Kyle Weintraub

INTERNS
Angela Bogart-Monteith
Taylor Kirby

CONTRIBUTING EDITORS
Robert Archambeau
Mark Brazaitis
Geoffrey Brock
A. Papatya Bucak
Victoria Chang
Martha Collins
Robin Ekiss
Tarfia Faizullah
V. V. Ganeshananthan
Kevin Haworth
Joy Katz
David Keplinger
Jesse Lee Kercheval
Jason Koo
Thomas Legendre
Randall Mann
Adrian Matejka
Pedro Ponce
Kevin Prufer
Frederick Reiken
James Richardson
Emily Ruskovich
Eliot Khalil Wilson

ART CONSULTANTS
Maria Elena Buszek
Adam Lerner

OFFICE MANAGERS
Maria Alvarez
Francine Olivas-Zarate

Copper Nickel is the national literary journal housed at the University of Colorado Denver. Published in March and October, it features poetry, fiction, essays, and translation folios by established and emerging writers. We welcome submissions from all writers and currently pay $30 per printed page. Submissions are assumed to be original and unpublished. For more information, please visit **copper-nickel.org**. Subscriptions are available—and at discounted rates for students—at regonline.com/coppernickelsubscriptions. *Copper Nickel* is distributed nationally through Publishers Group West (PGW) and Media Solutions, and digitally catalogued by EBSCO. We are deeply grateful for the support of the Department of English and the College of Liberal Arts & Sciences at the University of Colorado Denver.

CONTENTS

FICTION

NONFICTION

POETRY

TRANSLATION FOLIOS

On the Cover / Daisy Patton, *Untitled (To a fellow HHer)*
Oil on inkjet print mounted to panel, 24" x 18", 2015

(for more about Patton's work, visit daisypatton.com)

Editor's Note:

Congratulations to Analicia Sotelo, whose book *Virgin* was chosen by Ross Gay as the winner of the 2016 Jake Adam York Prize for a first or second poetry collection. Milkweed Editions will publish *Virgin* in February, 2018. Two poems from the book—"My Mother as the Face of God" and "Trauma with Haberdashery"—appear in this issue.

Finalists for the prize were Caylin Capra-Thomas, Kelly Davio, Dante Di Stefano, Charles Jensen, Jennifer Kwon Dobbs, Mia Malhotra, Bernard Matambo, Andrew McFadyen-Ketchum, Brianna Noll, Molly Spencer, Ryann Stevenson, Nomi Stone, Greg Wrenn, Jenny Xie, and Kim Young. All of these poets' books were brilliant, and, indeed, many of them are now forthcoming elsewhere.

An outstanding group of semifinalists were Nikia Chaney, John Lee Clark, Brian Clifton, James Ellenberger, Leah Falk, Landon Godfrey, Mark Gosztyla, Julie Hanson, Gary Jackson, Virginia Konchan, Tyler Mills, Chad Parmenter, Kate Partridge, Michelle Peñaloza, Vivian Faith Prescott, Corey Van Landingham, and July Westhale.

At *Copper Nickel*, we believe strongly in transparency. For virtually all book prizes, screeners do essential work toward choosing a winner, and too often their work goes unsung. For the Jake Adam York Prize, our policy is that all screeners must have published at least one book of poems. Our screeners for 2016 were Brian Barker, Nicky Beer, David J. Daniels, Sean Hill, Sara Michas-Martin, Emily Pérez, Chris Santiago, and myself. Big thanks to my colleagues for their attention and to Ross Gay for his difficult work in choosing a winner from an astonishingly good group of manuscripts.

The judge for the 2017 Jake Adam York Prize is Victoria Chang. The winner will be announced in early 2018.

In general, announcements about *Copper Nickel* and The Jake Adam York Prize are made throughout the year via the *Copper Nickel* website and social media. If you haven't already, please "like" us on facebook and follow us on twitter.

As ever, thank you for your support of *Copper Nickel* and, more generally, of literature and the arts, which are (as I'm sure you know, dear reader) essential to American culture and a healthy democracy.

—Wayne Miller

GRAHAM FOUST

Trigger Warning

There's a kind of enlisted prettiness flaking
away in these many places,
and it's like having been handed my hands,
this not-having-been-scared-enough-lately.
Germs leave worlds in me; flames close well-known roads and
even the seasons, immediately,
my failures next to language like a ditch
or sometimes in it like a bridge out, a trench.

On a good day, I fess up without remorse,
letting every formal model drift from dream to
near erasure; on a better one,
the grid willing, I lace my own and only life
like past affections, fled precedents,
gray light from some old film from some bad time.

Forward Slash

Having lived too late in this world and everyone else's,
about the sun, in the end, I'll do anyway what ice does—
stays if it must, or goes—and I'll expect the outdoors
but get instead a room, along with the "is"
in "missing," the "in" in "forgetting," a few feelings
believed in, but just beside the point of having with ease,
with speed, seen pieces of what can't happen, ideas
so fast that only years, if that, could get them back please.

ELIZABETH TANNEN

Dear Wisconsin

How can you be so sure of yourself, even here
in the curtain-clipped light of this Super 8 motel, miles from Madison—as if
you've got it all figured out? Don't you know we're in Sun Prairie,
Wisconsin! It's June
and I ate some of your strawberries—blotched
and ripe. I saw the bachelorettes crowd
your breweries. I tried to find new love, teetered
on an edge of this blemished bed, watched
glistered dreams collide
with logistics of morning. I remembered
the rains that draped the dash on the drive from New Glarus. I saw men
in suspenders dance the Polka; women celebrate
Beer, Bacon and Cheese. The Capital! We lapped its square
like we were re-making Ohio.
Remember Michigan? Don't you know it's bigger than you, and has more
intricate parts? Did you see the shade our faces made the moment
we woke up? Do you know what it's like to bleed between days
in your own sovereign state? In the Super 8 Motel
it's midnight and Shelley is smoking her tenth
cigarette of this Saturday night. *It's going to storm all day tomorrow*,
she's telling all the guests. Wisconsin,
she's going to be wrong.

SARAH CARSON

How to Baptize a Child in Flint, Michigan

First, hold the curve of his head
like packed snow, a struck match,

like a field mouse you promise
you'll let back into the grass.

Say he can be anything;
refill his root beer;
read him a story.

Say, "Yes, people like us can be great, too."

If you're going to the firehouse, bring him with you;

Tell him, "God is good,"
Even if the guardsman's cigarette
says God has lost control.

At home, dinner in the microwave,
Mountain Dew and TV light,

when the textbook
insists we are already water
say, "Of course, we are, boo,"

though you don't know the specifics,
just that Pastor says river is a holy thing;
Jesus himself could walk it in bare feet.

On Easter, when he falls asleep during the altar call,
when he wakes and whispers,
"What is brimstone? What's repentance?"

send him out to the narthex,
ask him if he's thirsty,

Tell him, "These reckoning songs
are not for us."

PETE STEVENS

When the Elephants Roam

DURING THE ELEPHANTS, MY FATHER died. He wasn't trampled underfoot or constrict-ed by trunk, and yet, either would've made more sense. The hospital representative, her nametag reading *Stephanie, Grief Specialist*, told me that he had passed in his sleep, peaceful. I said that it couldn't be true, that my father never slept. He would wander from room to room through the night, the morning, never finding sleep. Years back, when my mother was still alive, his nocturnal roaming was something of a curiosity, a sign of his eccentric nature. But recently, with my father living alone, I wanted him to be healthy and well rested, thought that the two went together. Stephanie again apologized for my loss and disappeared down the hallway. After missing their night of chess, a neighbor had entered his apartment to investigate and found my father slumped in his chair, apparently napping. The neighbor told me, you couldn't be sure with the state of the world these days, with wild animals taking to the streets. There was a chance, he said, god forbid, that my father had been eaten by an elephant.

•

ELECTRONIC MONITORING OF the perimeter failed. All the elephants escaped. Initial reports had them taking to the forested areas outside town, grouping in small herds, while others claimed that an elephant passed through their yard and drank from the pool. Melissa, my longtime and live-in girlfriend, wanted to see an elephant, wanted to touch one. I told her my father had died and she took a seat at the kitchen table. There, she began to peel an orange with the nail of her thumb. We sat together eating segments of the orange, its juices running down my fingers and wrist. We discussed the death rituals of elephants, how they touch their trunks to the dead and cry.

•

"I WAS SITTING in one of those orange plastic chairs shaped like an egg. They told me my dad's heart exploded," Melissa said. "Like a grenade, they said. I pictured—re-peatedly—a cartoon explosion erupting from his chest. The sounds even, *Boom, Boom, Boom*."

"How old were you?" I asked.

"Fourteen. And I know this sounds horrible, but I was a little relieved. I remember thinking that my mother and I could be alone now, and that somehow it would be better. My fourteen-year-old reasoning was that my mother and I could be closer, that my father wouldn't drag us around the country anymore."

"You didn't miss him?"

"Not then but I do now. I wish we could have a conversation, or even say goodbye. I was in gym class when I found out. We were playing volleyball."

•

MY FATHER'S APARTMENT had become a time capsule. All that remained of his life was this collection of items. Melissa and I were here for the deconstruction, the piece by piece erosion of his identity. Our plan was to keep as little as possible and donate the rest. First, I sat in his recliner, the one he died in. I closed my eyes and ran my fingers along the burgundy leather softened by years of his sitting. I expected to be hit with a flood of emotions and memories, but felt nothing. "Hey, James," Melissa said. "It's us." She held a framed photo of us holding hands at the base of a waterfall. There were photos of me as a child playing baseball. There were photos of my mother in the hayloft of a barn, looking happy, content even, and I didn't know where the barn was, nor could I place the year those shots were taken. There was a newspaper on the coffee table: "57 Elephants Escape from Nature Preserve." I read about Susan Bennett, a woman who could speak with elephants. They listened, she said. They understood, she said. Susan had opened an elephant preserve within the forested expanse of southern Georgia. She rescued elephants from circuses and bankrupt zoos. Once, years back, I drove up to the gates of the sanctuary and rolled down my windows to listen. Inside, the elephants swayed and ripped branches from trees. They called out to each other with blasts of great noise and I listened. Towards the end of the article, Susan implored everyone to use the utmost care and caution when encountering the elephants. Her children, she said, were missing.

•

"EVERYBODY WANTS WHAT they can't have," Melissa said. We were walking along the edge of the park, aimless. I asked her what she wanted. "An elephant," she replied, her arms rising to show how big. I said something about white elephants, about large and exotic animals making terrible pets. Think of the costs, I said. Think of the hassle. Then Melissa asked me, "Do you want to get married? Like ever?" And the only response I could think of was, *Why?*

•

WE STARTED AT the open gates of the preserve, then drove north into the forest on a desolate two-track road, where it was said the first elephant had been reclaimed. We parked and readied our provisions: water bottle, bird-watching binoculars, map, and compass. I studied the ground for signs, as if I knew a thing about tracking, hunting, or wildlife. I expected to see branches broken by the progress of herds, large stamps in the dirt. A lone dog—some sort of boxer/Doberman mix—followed us. The dog's eyes shone blue, then gold in post-dawn sunlight. He crisscrossed our path before breaking off to leave. His paws, I noticed, had made marks in the sandy dirt. "Maybe we should get a dog," Melissa said. This seemed more reasonable than a baby or an elephant. We continued through the woods with our map turned sideways and saw nothing but trees, the dirt path. Soon, the trees opened before us and off in the distance, maybe a half-mile, a shimmering lakeside came into view. I checked our map for the lake's name: Wixom. "Look!" Melissa said while grabbing the binoculars, not bothering to release the strap from my neck. "Elephants!" Yes. Through the binoculars, we watched two adult elephants drink water from the lake. We rushed towards the water, giddy. The elephants rose together and disappeared between trees.

•

"YOU DON'T THINK it's weird?" Melissa asked.

"No, it's weird. Definitely."

"I just remember all those cartoons growing up where the elephant was terrified of a mouse. So I'm supposed to believe that an animal weighing thousands of pounds would be afraid of a two-ounce mouse?"

"I think elephants are afraid that mice will run up inside their trunks."

"Seriously? That's why? Makes it seem even stranger, then. Why would a mouse want to run up an elephant's trunk? To stay warm?"

"Maybe. Or it could be that an elephant's skull makes a good home for a mouse. We'll never know."

•

THERE WERE MANY forms to sign. "Sign here, here, and here," the banker said. "And here." I signed them all. My father's assets transferred into my accounts with the ease of buying a mattress. "That's it?" I asked. "That's it, Mr. Brooks. Is there anything else you need?" What did I need? No, I said. In total, I became $74,000 richer. Now, the question: What did I want?

•

MELISSA TOLD ME that elephants could smell water from twelve miles away. She said that if we couldn't go to an elephant, then an elephant would have to come to us. In the center aisle, down from the BMX bikes, down from the Slip 'N Slides, I found a selection of kiddy pools stacked like plastic cups. The salesman sported a red vest and a moustache in need of a trim. "Hello, sir. May I help you?" I told him I needed a pool for my backyard. "How about this one?" The pool featured purple dolphins on its sides that appeared to be winking while they sprayed water from their blowholes. I had read one time, in some sort of zoological journal, that dolphins were one of the rare animals that had sex for pleasure. I'd also heard about a man who made love to a bottlenose dolphin in the low surf at a beach. The man said he stroked the dolphin gently, slowly gaining trust, until she rolled to expose her belly, her genital slit. Did elephants fuck for fun? I didn't know, couldn't picture the act in my mind. "How big is your child?" the salesman asked. I said, "As big as an elephant," and together we laughed. He directed me to the above-ground pools, pools that would require an afternoon to assemble. "Yes," I said. "I want the biggest one you have."

•

THE SUN FELL from the sky in a ball of orange and pink light. I stood and filled my pool with water from the hose. Five thousand gallons of water passed through my hose and into the pool, which had taken all day, and had, to my thinking, been a slow and sad process. Melissa and I had no intention of actually swimming in the pool, and we didn't bother to add chlorine, a filter, or pump. This pool, eighteen by eight feet in dimension, and uniformly four feet deep across, was a lure to lounge next to. Melissa climbed the ladder and peered over the edge. "Stop," I said. "It's not secure." She didn't listen and continued to stare at the water, her fingertips tracing the surface. Would my father, before his death, have wanted me to marry Melissa? I wasn't sure. I once overheard them discussing the prospect of grandchildren. Standing in my backyard, I could almost see two children, my son and daughter, playing in the pool. They'd be five and seven, splashing water, both held afloat by inflated tubes around their arms. I envisioned their smiles, their glee, then their open-mouthed shock as an elephant emerged from between the trees. The elephant went to the pool, saw my children, and plucked my son from the water with its trunk. I watched and let the elephant return to the woods. When Melissa said she was going inside to prepare dinner, I thanked her and followed.

•

LIKE MY FATHER, the two elephants appeared to be napping, peaceful. Closer inspection of the newspaper photograph revealed thin lines of blood streaming from beneath their bodies. The newspaper reported that a pair of elephants, Thomas and Lucy, had come into town looking for food or water, or both. They approached the public in anger, knocking over fruit stands, and the choice was made to put them down. Of the 57 elephants that initially escaped, 16 had been reclaimed or put down, and there was debate over the belief that all the elephants could be found. I hoped that they all wouldn't be found. I hoped that some would get free.

•

"GO!" MELISSA SAID. "Go!" Her words and hands were at my back, pushing. The clock read 2:48. I put on my robe, Melissa's hands still pushing, and took the steps downstairs two at a time. She had awakened from noises in the backyard, splashes from the pool. I turned the banister and made my way to the rear of the house. When I hit the lights, when a flood of yellow hit the backyard, I saw not elephants but two men, maybe teens, bare-chested in the pool. They turned to me, a look of surprise on their faces. "Hey!" I said. "What the hell?" Melissa came to my side and continued to push. I saw that they were not men, only boys. "We just wanted to go for a swim," one said, a hint of malice in his voice. Melissa stepped past me and told the boys to get out of the pool. She told them to get lost or she'd call the cops. *Relax, chill*, they said while descending the ladder. Standing face to face, I saw that these boys could deal me great harm. One was a head taller and the other had hands like shovels. I wanted to diffuse the situation. "We're leaving," Hands said. I looked away. Unfazed, Melissa rushed them along as they gathered their shirts and cigarettes, their cell phones and shoes. I was glad she had taken control. "Hey," I said after the boys were gone. "You're amazing." She walked past me and up the porch steps before turning to me. "Where were you? You think that's fun for me? Jesus, I'm shaking." And she was, her body flickering under the light like a candle flame. I stood in the grass, the shame of inaction growing. She was probably just upset. Upset that the boys were not elephants. Upset that her man would have been no help if they were.

•

MY FATHER MADE sure I wasn't a stranger to the gun. On lazy afternoons we'd go the range, under the sun, where he'd demonstrate the proper action for ejecting a shell. Shooting, I could handle. Football, I couldn't. I remembered tracing the arc of a clay pigeon through the sky with the barrel of my shotgun, the way a burst of orange flared against the clouds when I hit. "Yes, yes, yes," I said as Sherrie, the gun store owner, placed a gleaming rifle onto the countertop. Its polished wood looked slick, almost wet. "This here is the Winchester model 70, takes a .458 magnum. Big round." And it was perfect. I said I'd take it and Sherrie started the process.

•

SITTING ON MY couch at the end of the day, I chambered a round into the model 70 and then ejected the cartridge, relishing the precision of the gun's action. Chamber, eject. Chamber, eject. When Melissa returned home from work, where she served as an ER nurse, and was, according to her, basically an errand-runner for a team of egomaniacal trauma surgeons, she passed me on the way to the kitchen and didn't say a word. Chamber, eject. Chamber, eject.

•

"THEY'RE OUT THERE," I said.

"And?"

"So we should be, too. It's clear the pool isn't working. I propose we make a trip of it, a camping trip into the woods."

"Camping?" Melissa asked, with skepticism.

"Yes. Trust me. We can sleep in a tent and make fires. You said you wanted to take a trip to exotic locales, to see wild animals, and so we will."

"Hardly exotic and damn, James. You know I have to work. I can't take time off to go play in the woods. And when are you going back to work? Ever?"

"Jane said I could take my time getting back. She said I was in mourning."

"I bet she did. Are you going to bring the gun?"

"Yes. No doubt."

•

IT HAD BEEN two weeks since the initial escape. I watched the nightly news, read the backlog of papers, and combed the internet for any information about where the elephants had been reclaimed or put down. Then, with a map of our area spread flat on the kitchen table, I plotted the locations with a Sharpie. It reminded me of the dot-to-dot drawings I did as a child, where a page of seemingly unconnected dots became a picture of a lion or sports car by connecting the points in the correct order. As I continued to plot locations on the map, I almost expected the image of an elephant to present itself. Finished, I stepped back and stroked my chin. Melissa watched from the counter while opening a pomegranate with a large kitchen knife. The fruit's exposed seeds looked like wet rubies and I went to eat one. Together, we chewed on the tart fruit and discussed our plan. Melissa said she'd have two days free, which should be plenty of time to camp. I agreed, anxious to enter the woods with my gun. Later that night we watched on the news as a team from the sanctuary guided an elephant into the back of a military-looking truck. Susan Bennett, the founder, observed the process, looking concerned. I asked, "Could it really be that easy?"

•

"YOU'RE DOING IT wrong," Melissa said. I held a collection of metal rods that bent with their own weight. They didn't seem to fit as they should. We hiked the same path as before, where we had first seen the elephants, and decided to camp by the lake. My research with the map confirmed this destination and today the scene was picturesque: Georgia pines formed the edge of a deep and expansive forest. A field went on for miles, dotted with wildflowers, and straight ahead the lake surface rippled. Melissa and I studied the tent's instructions. "Here, here, it goes like this." "No, like this." Establishing the foundation, hammering the pegs into the ground, was easy enough, but not the construction of the roof and skylight panel. After another frustrated hour working together, and after three shared beers from an overstuffed cooler, the tent stood completed. We entered its caverns in awe: our own world, a bubble of comfort. On the left side of the tent, next to my sleeping bag, I set the plastic case for my rifle, and then opened it. She was beautiful. I closed the case and turned to Melissa: "Time for me to build a fire." Before we left the house, I had watched a video on YouTube on how to build a fire in the woods. Melissa looked on as I gathered tinder and constructed larger and larger frames, using sticks and branches from the woods. My movements displayed confidence. Five minutes later, I had what resembled a wooden teepee and lit the tinder below with a waterproof match. Fire. It came and it blazed. I sat back and basked in its radiance, in my own radiance. Together, Melissa and I positioned the metal apparatus I had bought at a camping store over the fire, designed for cooking. "It's perfect," Melissa said. That night we cooked T-bone steaks. We cooked baked beans and carrots wrapped in a tinfoil pouch. Drinking beers, as the fire snapped, sending sparks into the night, Melissa told me the story of a friend with a ball python. The friend got the snake when it was young and small but it grew fast. Melissa said that the snake had the run of the house, that it slept in the bed, always in a tight coil. Years later the snake started to sleep stretched-out next to her friend, elongated, now four-feet in length. Curious, the friend did some research and discovered that the python was sizing her up, waiting for the day it would be big enough to eat her. "Damn," I said. "That's fucked up." And yet, I understood. I was that snake, spending years to stretch out, elongate, waiting for the moment.

•

"No kid should ever have to see that," Melissa said. "It was only a few years before he died, so I must've been twelve. It messed with my head."

"How much did you see?"

"All of it. My mother, her face red and blotchy with stress, huffing and puffing. She was clearly suffering. Then my father panned to between her legs, which were splayed wide. There were doctors and nurses, and this was the eighties, so the video was grainy and poorly lit, the colors muted and somehow wrong."

"Sounds horrible."

"I know," Melissa said. "It was. My father said it was important for me to witness my own birth, my first seconds as an air-breathing human."

"Then there's this concept, where if you video an event, or take pictures, it's like you're not there, you only exist through the lens of the camera. The camera is there but you aren't. It's weird."

"Yeah, because then it was like my father wasn't even in the room, or if he was he served as some sort of reporter and not as a father or a help to my mother. If I had been her I'd be furious that he was recording this horrific process. I don't know why she let him do it."

"What did you say? Was your mother there when you watched it?"

"No, she wasn't. And I always hated my father for videoing the birth, for not being there for my mom."

"Hate is a strong word."

•

THE NEXT DAY we rose at first light and set out on foot through the woods. I carried my rifle in my hands, the chamber empty, using the barrel to push aside branches. A pair of cartridges tumbled in my pocket. The gun became heavy and sweat-slicked, and I told Melissa that I should've opted for a shoulder strap. We traversed through morning and into the afternoon, along paths and streambeds marked on my map. Melissa's hiking legs were strong, if not robust, and I didn't doubt that her stamina could outlast mine. I'd stop to take a drink of water from an upturned canteen. I'd stop to rest my aching arches. Melissa, always ready to push onward, was encouraging and uplifting. After hours of seeing only squirrels or birds, I doubted that we'd see any elephants. She couldn't or wouldn't agree. With the sun at its peak, we stopped for a lunch of granola and dried fruit. "Even if we don't see any elephants," Melissa said. "It feels good to get out and hike. I miss it." I told her that I agreed but didn't. I'd put too much stock in the idea of actually interacting with an elephant. With only a few hours of daylight left, we decided to make our way back to camp. I carried the rifle and chambered a round, weary of the coming darkness. Melissa held the binoculars. I wanted us to come upon a family of elephants, maybe drinking from a stream, maybe resting on their sides in the shade. We'd approach with caution and they'd let us run our hands along the slopes of their backs. They'd only snort from their trunks as we felt the knobs of their feet. Night came and Melissa held a flashlight, her beam focused and steady. When we reached camp, the beam caught two eyes looking back, unmoving. The dog, a feral Doberman, held one of the T-bones from our meal in its jaws. A second Doberman pushed his snout through our spilled cooler. In an instant, both of the dogs were barking, their teeth gnashing in the light. Melissa said something but I didn't hear her. I raised my gun a yard above their heads and pulled the trigger. I would always remember the burst of fire, the flash, the explosion of noise and the pain against my shoulder. Before the ringing in my ears stopped, before Melissa gasped in surprise, the dogs fled into the woods. "I couldn't shoot them," I said. "Never." Melissa touched my arm, my hand, and then said we should go home. I agreed. We cleaned and packed and within minutes we were back on the road, my foot on the clutch, shifting.

•

MELISSA PASSED BY me. I stopped on the porch and picked up the newspapers. Opening the first, I read about the elephants, how more than two-thirds of them had now been returned or shot down. Order, Susan Bennett said, was being restored. Then I heard the calls from Melissa: "James, James, hurry, come see!" Dropping the newspapers on the kitchen table, I went to her. In our backyard, two dusty-gray elephants were taking turns drinking from the pool. They'd dip the tips of their trunks in, splashing, seemingly carefree, and then they'd curl their trunks back to their mouths and spray the water in. We stood hypnotized by their loose and heavy movements. We listened to the low-pitched sway of their calls back and forth. "They look like toys," Melissa said. "Really big toys." I thought they looked like dinosaurs but knew that wasn't right. One of the elephants turned in our direction, almost knowing, as if looking right into my own eyes, but it never reacted or gave any indication of our presence. "We must be shielded," I said. "By the reflections in the glass." I didn't know if we should try and go outside, if we should risk it. Reading my thoughts, Melissa said we should stay where we were. "It's what we wanted. Stay here with me." And I did. I took her hand in my own and we watched. We'd never see another elephant again.

Translation Folio

LI QINGZHAO

Translator's Introduction

Wendy Chen

"MY THOUGHTS OF POETRY ARE like the magpie at night, / circling three times, unable to settle," writes Li Qingzhao (1084-1151) in one of her surviving fragments. Considered the greatest female poet in Chinese history, Li Qingzhao defied cultural expectations for women by mastering *ci* (lyrics), composing scholarly *wen* (essays) on a variety of subjects, writing political *shi* (poems) criticizing government policies, and gaining the acknowledgement of her male contemporaries for her literary and scholarly accomplishments.

As the daughter of a respected and prosperous family of scholar-officials, Li Qingzhao was both educated and encouraged in her literary pursuits. During her lifetime, she published several volumes of work under her pseudonym Yi'an Jushi ("the easily-contented dweller") and was recognized mainly for her *shi* and *wen*. Today, she is most celebrated for her oeuvre of *ci*—lyrics that matched existing songs with predetermined meters and tones. The titles of *ci* were frequently the titles of the songs they were set to, with the result of many *ci* sharing the same title. The actual musical scores of these songs, however, have been largely lost to history.

Much of Li Qingzhao's work has not survived—indeed very few *shi* and *wen* are available to us—and what has survived is plagued with questions of authenticity and attribution. In the dynasties following her death, editors who collected her works often discovered "new" pieces of hers in order to attract critical interest to their anthologies. Many of these hitherto undiscovered pieces were then folded into successive anthologies and accepted as part of her body of work. Thus, modern-day estimations of her remaining *ci* can vary widely depending on their source texts, anywhere from 40 to 80 or more.

Developed in the Tang Dynasty, *ci* was regarded as a popular genre, characterized by personal and romantic subjects rather than the loftier, political ones of *shi*. Though for the most part only men composed *ci*, they were often positioned from the point of view of a woman. Conventional subject matter included the lamentation of an unrequited love, the loss of beauty, or the passing of the seasons. Courtesans in entertainment halls would then perform and sing these *ci* for the appreciation of educated and wealthy men.

During the Northern and Southern Song dynasties, *ci* as a genre gained in popularity among literati, and thus acquired a more elevated status as an art form. It was during this flourishing period that Li Qingzhao composed her *ci* and became known for her deft turn of phrase, evocative imagery, and keen, observational eye. Although she rarely uses first or third person in her *ci*, her lyrics provide particular insight into the life of a woman of her position. "Alone, I look out of the window /," she writes, "into the black" ("Slow Notes").

Many of her *ci* follow conventions of the form in terms of their romantic subject matter, and has informed much speculation about her own life with her husband, Zhao Mingcheng, who was often away on scholarly and official business. Several unconfirmed anecdotes illustrate the popular understanding of their relationship as one founded on devotion, mutual love, and respect. In one, Zhao Mingcheng hides a poem of his wife's amongst a collection of his own, which he then shows to an esteemed literary friend for evaluation. After reviewing the poems, the friend declares all of them unremarkable except for one. This, of course, turns out to be Li Qingzhao's poem. Zhao Mingcheng, though frustrated as an artist in his own right, concedes her work is superior.

The inclination to exclusively interpret her work biographically is not without its issues. In his 2014 text *The Burden of Female Talent: The Poet Li Qingzhao and Her History in China*, scholar Ronald Egan examines the development of the literary criticism surrounding Li Qingzhao, focusing particularly on the ways her gender has informed such criticism.

Li Qingzhao also used the *ci* form to explore less conventional questions of exile, authorship, and artistic legacy. In 1127, the Jin invasion of Northern Song forced Li Qingzhao to flee south with the remainders of the court. She was greatly critical of the emperor's decision to withdraw rather than resist the invasion, and outwardly expressed her dissent in her writings.

Much of her later work thus incorporates themes of displacement and uncertainty. In "Picking Mulberries," the speaker is awakened by the sound of rain falling on banana tree leaves, a plant which grows only in the south. The sound, foreign to the ears of a "northerner," reminds her of her own foreignness and keeps her up at night. Li Qingzhao continues this theme in "Clear Serene Music," observing, also, her own mortality:

> This year, I stand at the edge
> of the earth.
>
> My temples white
> as the flowers.

Scholars and artists in the generations following her death have acknowledged her as a master of her craft—a status few women have ever achieved in Chinese history. Yet despite her distinguished reputation in China, she remains relatively unknown and untranslated in the West. Only one translation of her complete works in English remains in print today (Rexroth, 1980). Gender, I believe, plays no small part in this neglect. Having first translated her *ci* in 2011, I am currently working on a more complete and accurate translation of her collected poetry. As part of my project, I am also interested in reclaiming Chinese/English translations as a space where Chinese and Chinese-American voices can be heard and appreciated.

In "Longing," Li Qingzhao asks, "Who will drink with me / from wine and poems?" My translations will, I hope, revive interest in her work and bring a new audience to her writing.

LI QINGZHAO : Five Poems

Clear Serene Music

Year after year, I stood in the snow,

drunk, always cutting the branches
of plum blossoms.

Crushing the flowers
for no good reason

until my clothes were filled
with all their dew.

This year, I stand at the edge
of the earth.

My temples white
as the flowers.

I feel the evening wind blow in.

Tomorrow, it will be difficult
to see the plum blossoms.

Picking Mulberries

Who planted the banana tree
in front of the window?

Its shadows fill the courtyard.
Its shadows fill the courtyard.

Leaf. Leaf.
Heart. Heart.

They unfold and fold again,
spilling over with emotion.

Pained, I listen
from my pillow
to the midnight rain.

The unceasing, heavy rain,
the unceasing, heavy rain,

hurts me,
a northerner, a stranger
to rising and hearing the sound.

Silk-Washing Stream

I am too lazy with spring
to comb again
my undone hair.

The evening wind in the courtyard.
The first plum blossoms fall.

Pale clouds come and go,
smudging the moon.

The incense rests
in the jade duck censer.

The tasseled curtains,
red as cherries,
are drawn over the bed.

Can rhinoceros horn still
ward off the cold?

Longing

Warm rain. Sunny wind. The ice
begins to break.

Willow eye. Blossoming cheek
of plum.

Already, I feel the heartbeat of spring.

Who will drink with me
from wine and poems?

Tears dissolve my face powder.

The inlaid flowers in my hair
are heavy.

I try on the jacket stitched with gold.

I lean my head against the pillow,
crushing the phoenix hairpins.

Alone, I carry the pigment
of sorrow.

I do not have good dreams.

Deep into the night,
I am still trimming the lamp's
flowery wick.

Slow Notes

Searching, searching. Seeking, seeking.
Cold, cold. Blank, blank.
Icy, icy. Misery, misery.
Grief.

Warmth is first, but brief.
Even longer—the cold season.

There is no peace for me.

Two or three cups of weak wine
can't stand against the scraping, evening wind.

The wild geese also leave,
also tear me,
though we were once friends.

The yellow flowers heaped on the ground—
I am too weak to gather them.

Alone, I look out of the window
into the black.

The rain falls doubly on the wutong tree,
drop by drop until dusk.

All this,

how could one word—"sorrow"—
ever be enough?

translated from the Chinese by Wendy Chen

ASHLEY KEYSER

The Enlightenment

The woman cramming offal offspring up herself knew, as did we all,
to be a successful freak was *work*. Those garbled ersatz monsters
she flushed, squatting, into a bucket—eel spines, tabby paws, a cull
of seventeen wee bunnies—roused England to a revulsion
it savored, at least till piqued by the Age of Reason's next horror-
of-the-month. Spectacle glutted them: furry girls like pampered
kittens in bonnets, or the man whose mute twin dangled, eyes always
shut, out of his chest. Not enough, not to have arms or legs, so one
Buchinger trained his delicate fins to engrave, pipe a tune, and caress
his brace of mistresses, whose nethers bawds dubbed "Buchinger's
boots." Meanwhile, giants stooping into London's doorways
grew ever taller, depending on whom you asked and how fierce
the competition. When I was the Irish Giant, I sprung up from 7'7"
to 8'2" to 8'4," whatever length of me cloaked in yards-long velvet
billowing as I strode like a pleasure-ship's sails. They said I lit
my pipe on streetlamps and kept a dwarf paramour, but their gossip
meant bread in my mouth, so I met my gawkers gratefully,
sleepy in my manners as a worn hillock. But never going home
from the circus, carrying it, rather, in one's person, is a weight
greater than any myth-man, and no bulk can shoulder it long.
While my fans, agog as carp, drifted to upstarts trumpeting
their advantage of a few inches, I grew sicker, drunker, terrified
of surgeons' knives at my corpse. In the end, they'd haul me
out of my coffin that ought to have sunk to the seabottom,
chop me up and boil me down to my bones, which now hang—
like a brute Viking's trophy, his conquered titan of a rival—
at the Royal College of Surgeons, for the edification of the crowds.

KEVIN PRUFER

The Committee on Village Security

We locked him in a cage
and hung that cage from an old tree
down the hill from the village gate

just out of reach of the zombies
who nightly gathered below him
sucking their teeth and wailing.

He smelled good to them
and thus distracted them
from climbing the hill

and attacking us where we slept.
Mornings, we fed him and
once each week, we lowered his cage

and hosed him off. He had been
nothing but trouble to us,
and this seemed like a fair way

of putting a member
of the criminal class
to work for the public good,

though soon enough
the scent of him (and the simple fact
of vanishing populations in the hills)

brought more zombies to our gate.
Another cage was required,
which we filled and hung

from another tree in the valley.
This seemed a sort of mercy.
By day the criminals might

offer each other
a measure of solace or company,
communicating across the grassy distance,

and by night, their presence
ensured security and quality of life
for those of us in the village above them.

This was long ago.
You were young
and probably don't remember

when the village wasn't ringed
by dozens of cages. And if we have been,
of late, less solicitous

for their inhabitants'
cleanliness and welfare,
it is because these times demand it.

By necessity, we are now
a smaller population.
But, as a result, we also grow

increasingly decent
with every criminal we put to use.
Of course there are ethical considerations,

we take your point.
But the sun sets every night in the valley
and we can't avoid certain grim necessities,

even as we welcome all
dissent, productive or not.
Please, rest assured—

we have the community's welfare in mind,
no matter what you say,
no matter what is in your secret thoughts.

JEHANNE DUBROW

Self-Portrait with Cable News, Graffiti, Weather

When I see the woman on TV, so calm
in her porcelain-white suit, I remember
that I too smiled while a man talked over,
that I bore the persistent tar of his voice.
In those meetings, I watched the veins
in his face like cracks in a disappointed street.
Were it not for his cruelty, I might have said,
I'm sorry for your loss. Who knows.
That year, my husband would overhear me
talking in my sleep, and though he couldn't open
the shut door of dreaming, he told me that I said,
fuck you, into the dark. Quite clearly, *fuck you.*
Night and waking were locked rooms,
the only exit a stuck window, and the heat
was always going or the cold. *Next order of business,*
a colleague said. I noted every conversation—
on the page, no one interrupted. Often,
remembering that year, I hold a serving bowl,
touch its surface limned with flowers, this thing
I've dropped or knocked against a shelf,
the way it refuses, decorative, to break.
Now I can say *fuck you* quite clearly to that year,
although there was also the kindness of friends
who brought over cherries—they knew
I loved the sweetness of a stone. I can say *fuck you.*
I will not lose the taste for it. In that year,
I was, truth be told, willing to punch a fist
through glass if it meant escape. I walked
down Greenwood Avenue, past the house
where someone had sprayed FUCK YOU
on the road and someone else had tried to X it out,
pale lines on top of lines. I understood
wanting to write one's fury on a place.

I understood even the impulse to erase it,
walking each day across the purity of imperative,
how it disturbed the concrete silence.
Most of us are not the woman on TV
who keeps talking, while the man is shouting
wrong into a mic—she keeps talking while
he stands beside her like a mugger in an alleyway
and who knows what he wants to take.
Most of us are the audience watching the debate—
we comply when the moderator says *no applause,*
no interruptions please. Most of us wait for night
to write FUCK YOU on a clean patch of asphalt.
All of this to say I could have said much more.
I could have written something on the man's sad face
and walked across my speech. FUCK YOU.
I think of him. I think of Greenwood Avenue,
its unremarkable houses that I learned to hate—
always moving towards a meeting or
coming late from one. I think of the sound
that spray paint makes, the rattle-shake of the can,
the aerosol's soft hiss, the words emerging
slowly on a path, jagged perhaps, but large
enough, remaining legible through rain.

PETER LaBERGE

Broadcast: Morning After

On the radio, the psychotherapist said

       queer boys were on the road
to hell. My mother & I were driving

       across town to church, where—
with any luck—my faith

       would finally hatch. I was
twelve. Upon hearing this news

       I knocked the small nest
I'd spent my life building

       from the branch & it dropped
obediently down my throat. The egg

       began its life-long wait—for years
I filled its nest with forbidden

       thoughts & dared the guilt
to come. But in every dream

       I woke from the touch
of a knife-tip to the stomach,

       as close to life as I was
far. The knife

       was guilt making itself
known. There was no nest

for equidistant boys. No nest, no name—

I called my body *morning*
because it was & each day

it was here my life began.

SHARA LESSLEY

Plausible Deniability

One day my daughter
will ask if
          I believe in heaven,
if darkness
calls us
          to lives beyond
this flesh. Lord,
why did you
          save us
from the sea, the rain,
                    but leave us
these borders,
your map of stones
          intact? Scattered
across the hard-
wood floor: her plastic
                    saints and fish.
She'll want to know
what the skies
          hold, what happens
when the winds
retreat. How can I
tell her what
          I've seen? In cold
clear air, our Father
          God like a bird
of prey, circling
                    then gone.

The Long Flight Home

Amman to Washington D.C.

Forget what I said about the black iris. I thought the national
bird was the hawk. I expected mostly to touch something
Holy, to see the Dead Sea scrolls locked in a temperature-
regulated box. For years I toured the Cardo's sacred precinct,

totally clueless. When *pleasing* came out *Halloween*, the florist said
Speak English. I'm still baffled by the military quartet bagpiping
in the ruined temple. Don't ask me about the intifada. Don't ask
who stashed the Russian ammunition in Irbid's tombs. There are

dissertations on why farmers turn bombers, why Bedouin
adorn bridal caps with cowries and coins. Autumn reshuffled
her cards. Arab Spring began that December, *First Noel*
blasting through the Palestinian bakery. Don't ask me why

thousands chanted support for the King while the Brotherhood
made the papers. What do I think of His Majesty? They say
he's the Prophet's descendent. They say he poses as a cabbie
to glean what people think. Don't ask me whether I've prayed

in a taxi. I was mostly wrong about women. I was mistaken
about men who deal arms. I've seen the High Altar of Sacrifice,
doubt Salim was slain. Forget what I said about the maid
locked in the apartment above us. I assumed her cries were

the wife's—some ordinary marital strife. Forget the sound
in our common courtyard, white washcloths dropped like
swifts. Her employers seized her passport, phone, held her
wages. The national bird's a rosefinch; the national tree, a sub-

species of oak. One night, something like furniture breaking. I woke in a fog. Forget the sidewalk, the rail from which she leapt to the carport below. I expected to touch something holy. Her femur, shattered the x-ray would show. The chapter on

faith says not long ago it was custom horses tramp the backs of believers who lay in the street like dogs. It says distance clarifies misunderstanding. I'm told the human plank would hold.

JOANNA PEARSON

Rumpelstiltskin

BREE BEGAN TO DREAM THAT the doctor was placing a small, silvery fish inside her, always with the promise that it would turn, eventually, into a human baby—a tiny version of her husband and herself, their darling replica. In the dream, she could see that the doctor held a minnow, or possibly one of those iridescent fishing lures her father had used throughout her childhood. She remembered the fishing lures as dangerous objects of great beauty, tantalizing her with their feathers, their shimmering gunmetal greens and dragonfly blues. They lay nestled in her father's tackle box like jewels, barbed hooks just waiting to snag flesh. *Noli me tangere.* In the dream, Bree would wince at the moment of insertion but the doctor always spoke in such a calming voice that Bree felt reassured. This was how babies were made, scientifically speaking. You stuck in a fish, like the Thanksgiving Indians had done when planting corn. Fertilization. She remembered some fact like this from elementary school so when the dream-doctor explained it this way, it made a certain sense. She would wake from this dream with the pleasant sensation of having taken definitive action toward a goal.

The point of the dream was that Bree was willing. She was willing to do it all. Stick fish or fishing lures up inside herself, suck down protein smoothies and wheatgrass, purchase healing crystals and naturopathic supplements, take special yoga classes. Pinch an inch of belly fat and inject herself with supra-physiologic doses of hormones each evening. Inject progesterone into her buttocks until they flowered with soft, lavender bruises. Say jump, she'd say how high.

And so far, nothing. You pay money like that and you expect something.

Bree had a good job, but not *that* good a job. The same was true for her husband, Owen. This was not a thing they did lightly. She'd stopped counting at this point—all the cycles, all the failures, all that money dumped into a gaping pit.

A friend of a friend of Bree's had been in a support group in which a woman announced she was planning to write a humorous memoir about the whole experience entitled "Inconceivable!" Bree had laughed when her friend, Lisa, told her this story not because the book title was funny, but because it wasn't. It was exactly the sort of sour anecdote she craved. She had just seen another pregnant woman pass and felt a convulsion of jealousy—these pregnant women, so shameless with their big, brazen bellies! Rubbing it in everyone else's face. Meanwhile, here was Bree, her uterus rattling around like a dried gourd.

Lisa was the one person Bree could confide in, and they'd already talked through all the acupuncture recommendations, massage therapists, specific brands of Coenzyme Q, and the SART success rates for the various reproductive endocrinology clinics. Lisa had finally, after years of frustration, had a baby herself, and she emerged now from the cloister of new motherhood more tired-looking and less triumphant than Bree would have imagined. The baby was at home napping with his father, and Lisa whispered this like it was scandalous. Babies, they consumed you. Literally. Lisa had the hollowed look of someone fleeing disaster.

"There's one thing you still haven't tried," Lisa said, stirring her coffee carefully with a spoon. Her eyes when she looked up at Bree were those of either a prophet or a lunatic. "The thing that finally worked for us."

Lisa looked side to side to see if anyone else was in earshot, then whispered so that Bree had to lean closer to hear.

"It's not scientific or anything, but we have Hartley now. I've still got the phone number."

Bree was nodding so furiously she couldn't focus.

"Please. Anything."

Lisa paused, frowning slightly. She seemed to hesitate before pulling out a crumpled yellow paper from her bag and passing it to Bree.

"I can't quite explain it to you. I mean, I couldn't if I wanted to, but I'm also not supposed to."

Lisa looked apologetic, but Bree merely nodded. She would call. She would do anything. Make every bargain, give up what she had to give up, sell what she had to sell.

Bree grabbed the sticky note and stuck it in her pocket.

"Thank you," she said. "Thank you."

Some kind of hocus pocus. Fertility spells. She could accept that. It was no weirder than the rest of it. She would go deep into the forest, to the witch's house. She would do all of it, without complaint. Whatever it took.

•

THE PROBLEM WITH Owen was that he was a good man, a decent man—a man of faith, even. This had been exactly what had drawn Bree to him in the beginning. She knew herself, knew the sharp edges of her own longings, well enough to know that she would benefit from matching herself with a more generous soul. Placid. Owen had a placid quality. He had the same eyes one saw on faces in old, religious triptychs—not the faces of the martyrs, eyes turned heavenward in holy subjugation, but the faces of the observers, the ones who stood there calmly and said to themselves, *Well, I suppose this is how it's all meant to be. I suppose this is just the divine plan.*

Owen taught at a very competitive private school—the school to which they could send their hypothetical child, for free, unless overcome with conscience. They lived in a pleasant neighborhood where people owned nice things but tempered this with an appropriate measure of guilt. Little girls in the neighborhood had truck-themed birthday parties and little boys were given gifts of baby dolls, and parents took their toddlers to vigils in the name of causes righteous and good. Owen's school was the same way— he loved teaching there. He had a gift for it. He also volunteered on weekends. He was very handsome, to boot; people said he looked like Jon Hamm. The only person people said Bree looked like was her mother.

"I'm happy with things as they are," Owen had told her, had been telling her from the beginning. "But I'll support you. We'll play this thing out as far as you want. All the way to the end."

Bree had just thrown a small temper tantrum over having to make a meal for the couple up the street who'd just had a baby. They got the baby *and* the homecooked meals?! It seemed grossly unfair.

"Of course it's not fair," Owen responded evenly, splashing balsamic vinegar onto the salad he was finishing in its Tupperware bowl. "The world isn't fair. Look, look at all we have here."

He gestured to their home, which was, Bree had to admit, nice enough. She had a nice home and a nice husband; meanwhile, people were getting shot by police officers, and police officers were getting shot by snipers, and children were being kidnapped and forced to be child soldiers, and refugees were drowning in their flimsy boats before they could make it ashore, and the last hospital for miles was getting bombed in Syria. Just yesterday, she'd seen a heartbreaking photo of an injured child in Aleppo, soot-covered and staring. The list went on. And yet so clearly was she focused on her own particular grievance with the universe that these greater woes did little to make Bree feel appreciative. All of it just made her even sadder. *Farewell, little no-baby, it's a bad-sad unfair world anyway.*

Owen snapped the lid on the salad and pulled out a loaf of bread from the oven with his mitts. He'd made the whole dinner for the couple up the street himself while she'd sulked.

Bree watched him and found herself inexplicably hating his goodness, his even temper. It was lonely to be so miserable by herself. She wanted to drag him down into the murky depths of her sadness like a mermaid drowning a sailor.

Her friend had warned her about this: a want like this could strangle a marriage. There was an art to managing thwarted expectations. The whole thing made Bree hate herself— at least the twisted version of herself she'd become.

"I'll practice gratitude," she said, wanting very much to mean it. "I want to be grateful for all these things. For our good life."

And Owen smiled at her so thankfully that she wished her heart was more authentic. She wanted to be the woman he deserved.

"My sweetheart," he said, pulling her toward him, kissing her and then nuzzling the back of her neck.

The paper Bree's friend had given her seemed to burn in her pocket, alive with a kind of animate heat. She felt false, self-conscious, and pulled away from him.

"We may still get our good luck yet," she said.

"We've already had such good luck," he said, not unkindly. "No matter what. Remember?"

•

THE WOMAN'S HOUSE, when Bree drove up to it, was set back from the road down a long gravel drive. She'd had to drive out into the adjacent county, a good twenty minute drive. Bree passed a farmhouse, and then a stable advertising horse riding lessons. She passed a little white house with a wide porch. Rustic. That was the word. Bree could imagine the sort of woman she was going to meet: an older woman with smile lines at her eyes who smelled of homemade bread, someone who knew homeopathic remedies and had herbs drying in her kitchen. The thought comforted her.

When Bree pulled up to the address, she saw that the house was bigger than she'd expected but also more run-down. There was a visible sag to the roof and a brown speckled couch losing its stuffing sat in the front yard.

Bree parked and walked to the front door, but before she could even knock, someone opened it.

"Yvonne?" Bree said, blinking from the bright day into the dimness inside. "I'm here for Yvonne."

But the person opening the door was a child, a scraggly little boy wearing shorts but no t-shirt. His chest and abdomen were practically concave, and his scapulae protruded sharply like denuded wings.

He nodded to Bree and beckoned her inside.

The interior of the house had a damp, ammonia smell. As her eyes adjusted, Bree realized there were cats crouched everywhere: an orange tabby perched atop a shelf, a black and white cat sleeping in one corner, a fat brown cat darting under her feet. There were heaps of things everywhere—junk, as far as Bree could tell. Piles of fabric, empty boxes, a grandfather clock open to the guts as if someone had tried to fix it but then abandoned the job.

Bree paused, taking it all in, and the boy mistook her hesitation for admiration.

"Mama collects things to sell on eBay," he explained, his voice lower than she'd expected. He gestured to an old stereo with a large dent in the side.

Bree nodded, almost tripping on what turned out to be a toddler.

"That's Maisie," the boy explained. "Scoot, Maisie. Get out of the way."

Maisie wobbled away on chubby legs, heavy diaper sagging.

The house was hot and stagnant, and it gave Bree a queasy feeling. She began to second-guess her decision to come here. Maybe she'd found the limits of what she was prepared to do.

When the boy opened the back door, she was relieved. He led them to a cement patio upon which sat a large, inflatable pool. After the dimness inside, it was too bright. Bree squinted. More children, more cats. The cats skittered and skirted her feet, and the children dashed around barefoot, calling to one another. A couple of younger children splashed in the pool where, presiding over the scene, sat a large woman in a flowered one-piece on a plastic raft. She floated, immense and queenly, over to Bree, waving to her like an old friend.

"Well, hey," she said, as if they were old friends. "You made it."

Bree wet her lips before answering. She needed a glass of water.

"Hi," she said. "You must be Yvonne."

The woman nodded.

"You want a baby," Yvonne said. She had on large, heart-shaped sunglasses, but Bree could sense Yvonne assessing her from behind the shaded lenses. "No luck so far, huh?"

"None," Bree saidd. "My friend, Lisa, said you could help."

"Oh, yeah," the woman responded calmly. "Gonna cost you, though. A thousand bucks. Then you get your baby, guaranteed."

Bree wanted to laugh with relief. A thousand dollars was a bargain at this point! She'd paid for prescription medications that cost more.

Bree was already pulling out her checkbook when the woman put a wet hand on her arm. She pushed the heart-shaped glasses atop her head so that Bree could see her eyes, which were tired and brown but winning, like a loyal dog's.

"Before you pay," she said. "You should know up front. No backsies, no refunds, no blabbermouthing."

Bree nodded furiously.

"Of course," she said. "As long as I get a baby. My own." She felt nervous all of a sudden.

Yvonne nodded, pulling down the sunglasses again. With one hand, she paddled her float over to the other side of the pool where a glass of what appeared to be lemonade sat. She took a drink.

"Write it out to Y.B. Miller Plumbing," she said. "It's the hubby's business, so." She flung a hand to the side as if indicating her absent husband.

Bree was already writing the check. The woman smiled.

"Give that to Horace," she said, and as if by magic, the skinny, shirtless boy had appeared beside Bree.

Bree awaited further instruction, or to be handed some potion or poison.

"That's it," Yvonne said, chuckling. "It's already in motion. Whether you like it or not. Millie, come show this lady back around to her car."

A scrawny girl-child emerged from the other side of the pool where she must have been crouched, playing in a patch of dirt. Obediently, she walked over to Bree and made a practiced mock-curtsy.

There were even more children, Bree realized. She blinked. The longer she stood there, the more they seemed to emerge like camouflaged moths from a patterned background. She noticed now another little shirtless boy in overalls standing by the side of the house where he seemed to be assisting another larger boy, hunched and stooped. They seemed to be working at something—a stretch of gutter or a bit of siding on the house—and it was only when the hunched boy turned to look at Bree that she realized she was staring. Something about the angle of the sun made the boy look deformed and ancient, with a leering old man's face. He wore a jagged silver chain of sorts around his neck that caught the sun, sparkling like knives. He winked knowingly at her—she could have sworn he did—and she turned quickly away. It was nothing. A trick of the sun.

"How will it work?" Bree asked. "How will I know?"

"You'll know."

Yvonne began to paddle to the other side of the pool, and Bree knew her audience was over. The afternoon was too bright and she had a sharp pain behind her eyes. Millie, scrawny and mute, tugged at the hem of her shirt. Bree followed the girl back around to the front. She was trembling slightly when she tried, at last, to start her car.

•

WHEN NOTHING AT all happened in the coming days or weeks, Bree was not surprised. As soon as she'd gotten home, any illusions she'd held about her visit to Yvonne's had vanished. Another thousand dollars lost: at this point, pocket change. She wouldn't tell Owen. She'd cut corners in other ways, make frugality her penance.

"You should have married Clara," Bree said to Owen yet again one evening. It was her preferred form of self-torture. Clara had been the long-term girlfriend who preceded her. Clara, perfect, golden-limbed Clara, with her three beautiful children and gentle husband. Bree and Owen were still friendly with Clara and her husband. Lovely, non-jealous Clara. Kind, fecund Clara.

Bree was leaning into their bathroom mirror digging at an angry red bump on her chin, and it felt painful and correct: something Clara would never do. Smiling, un-blemished Clara. She would become the anti-Clara. Another form of self-abnegation, another punishment.

Owen put down his toothbrush and sighed. He'd made some reassuring remark to this statement at least fifty times before.

"Bree," he said. "Look at me."

And she turned to him, catching the full reflection of the two of them in the mirror now: Owen's even, handsome face; her own, with her tired eyes, her chin angry and inflamed.

"Stop it," he said softly. "Please. You have to stop it."

And she did not answer him, but later she cried. She cried because she knew it was true: she should stop but she couldn't. She'd made herself into the dark fairy at the christening, her heart an ugly knot of brambles. She'd formed a bad habit she now inhabited so deeply it was unbreakable.

A few weeks later, Bree saw Lisa at the local food co-op with baby Hartley strapped to her chest in an Ergo. Lisa's husband, Richard, was nearby, testing the ripeness of the avocados, while Lisa trailed her fingers over the lettuce. The first moment Bree saw them, she felt a pang of jealousy—Lisa had left her behind and joined the club of mothers, and now, here she was, perfect husband and baby in tow. A pretty picture. But you could swallow your own bitterness, Bree had found. You could swallow it, and it was poison, but it was a poison you became used to, by degrees. So she swallowed and moved toward them to say hello.

But there was something wrong. Bree hesitated, watching them from a display of cheeses, trying to figure out what it was.

They weren't speaking. She realized this now. They wore the silent faces of the stricken, the stunned. Even Baby Hartley. His small mouth hung slack, and although his eyes were open, he seemed dully unaware of his surroundings. Richard wore a similarly glazed expression. Lisa lifted a head of lettuce and placed it in their basket. When her arm brushed Richard's, he seemed to shudder involuntarily and pull away.

Things were not right. Bree could see it clearly now: a sort of sickness had befallen them. She stared at them, their ordinary faces gone monstrous in the produce section lighting, then backed away.

Bree fled, hurrying to the exit on the other side of the store. She left without the milk or the cheese or the special local jam she'd intended to pick up. She left with nothing but a heavy sensation encompassing her whole chest. She was feverish, queasy.

Bree couldn't quite catch her breath the whole ride home. A cloud passed over the sun, and she felt an incipient sense of dread. She would make things better. She had to. She would start by making dinner for herself and Owen. They would eat together. They would sit on the porch with drinks the way they used to, and he would tell her funny stories from his day. They hadn't done this, not for so long. Owen would remember to squeeze just the right amount of lime for her. She would kiss him and knead the knot he always got on the right side of his shoulder. They would laugh. She couldn't remember, now that she thought about it, the last time they'd so much as smiled at one another.

When she pulled up to the house, there was a battered old truck parked up front although they were not expecting anyone. Something fluttered in her, but she took a deep breath. At the door, fumbling for her keys, she could hear voices inside. Owen's and a stranger's.

She entered the house and walked to the kitchen. A man sat with his back to her at the table across from Owen. She saw that Owen had poured them both glasses of iced tea. Owen caught her eye. He was looking at her in a new way. The muscle of his jaw flickered, but he pressed his lips into a tight line. Unreadable.

"Bree," he said, and his voice had such a practiced calm that it chilled her. "We have a guest."

She frowned. The visitor, whose back still faced her, was a small man. He looked older, too thin. Emaciated, really. There was a hitch to his shoulders, an unevenness she could see from where he stood. His hair curled on his neck in oily ringlets. She caught Owen's eyes again and shook her head furiously, but he just held her gaze, implacable.

"Come on over and sit down," Owen said, rising from his seat. "He's explained it all. We'll play this thing out. All the way to the end."

She took a breath and stepped forward, careful not to look at the visitor directly.

"No, Owen," she said, but her voice came out very weakly, like a whimper. "This isn't what I meant."

"I'll let him introduce himself," Owen said, picking up the jacket he'd draped across the back of the chair. "I'll let you two talk." He was leaving now, Bree realized. He was leaving her alone with the strange man.

Owen put on his jacket and moved around the table toward the door. She caught his arm, her fingers digging into the flesh, but he jerked away, rougher than she'd ever known him to be with her.

Bree stood, immobilized, next to the visitor sitting at her table. She could see him in profile in her peripheral vision. He was not a man, no, not really. She saw the odd hump to his back, his concave chest, and suddenly, he was very familiar to her. The body of a misshapen boy, the face of a wicked old man. She could not bear for him to look at her. She could not bear to look at him directly. He cracked his knuckles, and she saw each of his hands, knobby and calloused but strangely adorned. Each of his fingers were knobbed with unusual silver rings, each sharp and geometric, spiky in their stalagmite-complexity.

"Please don't leave, Owen," she whispered.

Owen stood, pale, watching her from the doorway. She wanted to throw her arms around him, she wanted to cry out. But she stood there, saying nothing.

The man at the table gave a slight nod, and Owen looked to Bree, as if for confirmation—she thought that if she could just call the whole thing off, they might still go back to how they'd been before. But she did not. It was irrevocable. She knew that by now. Owen's face tightened and he turned from her.

Too late, Bree whispered, "Wait."

But by then, Owen was already gone, the door to their beautiful house clicking softly shut behind him, and she was left with her this troll, this manikin, who turned slowly to look at Bree, lifting his glass of tea as if making a toast (and she could see now that he was vain in his way, with the manicured fingers of a dowager).

"I don't know you," Bree said, her mouth gone completely dry. "I don't know you at all. You shouldn't be here." She sank to the chair next to him, though, so close that she could hear the faint whistle of his breathing.

The little man just looked at her peaceably with his pitted cheeks and toothless grin. His touch was damp and cool, but she let him take her hand. When he rose, she followed him.

ALEX McELROY

Surrender

M AND I MARRY IN the desert under the watch of hawks nesting in a cactus. Shotguns are shot out of sight. We crouch at the sound, cover our heads. After the wedding we move to Bulgaria, where M will teach American English to teenagers. Where I will be known as the spouse. On our second day in the country we attend a meeting where a former marine tells us and 24 other American teachers what we should fear: alleys, emails, migrants, ISIS, organized crime ("The OC"), kidnappers, and habits. He is tall, righteously chummy, his hair stiffer than wood. He demands that we vary our routes when we walk: "You must know you don't know who knows your routines." This segues into sexual violence: "Nobody likes to talk about it—but me." For ten minutes he toes the edge of the subject. "It can happen to men," he finally, triumphantly says, "Don't think I don't know it can happen to men." After the meeting M and I fuck in our hotel room. We wash our clothes in the shower then hang them to dry. Wet socks like flattened fish on the lampshades, pants sizzle steamily on the radiator, bras drip suds from the blades of a fan. M hangs a white shirt out the window. Flapping, its arms tap on the glass. That night a revolving door nearly severs my head. It does not, of course, but it nearly does, and now when I think of my neck, soft as a plum, hovering between the propelling door and its jamb, I don't remember what happened— my twitch into safety—but I remember those few slippery seconds spent gazing up from the floor, watching M fall over my body. We both suspect we will die in Bulgaria and spend our free time conjuring how it will happen. Esophageal cancer, aneurysm, tuberculosis, a bombing. When anxious I mutter with my favorite Bulgarian phrase, *Za'mnogo godini*: "May you continue living." In Sofia a monument shaped like a head sits on a black beveled stone. A gash the length of a child runs from the crown to the mouth. For months I assume the gash is a mark of urban decay. But the subject, I discover, died split by a saber. A lesson? Perhaps: What responsibility do artists have to the actual? My chest tightens. When I breathe I feel as if ropes are binding my ribs. I schedule an appointment with an English-speaking doctor in Sofia. In his office, a signed photograph of the doctor posing with Sylvester Stallone hangs on the wall. This puts me at ease. When I tell him my chest has been hurting he tells me that Gypsies are taking over his country. A police officer briefs M and me on possible threats to our safety. He doesn't speak English. When he talks I hear the few Bulgarian words that I know—*neshto*, *tuk*, *tova*—each like the flash of a face on a TV fuzzy with static. Our translator tells us he tells us not to be scared of the migrants. We hadn't brought up the subject. "They do not stay here. They are looking," he says with a smirk, "for a better life." A man in a café stares at M and me as we eat. *Amerikanski*, he says, waving his hand to rally the people around him. They leave. He gets up to smoke. Relieved, we are for a second, then spot him in the window watching us talk. We bolt when he goes to the bathroom. M's students think we are spies. "We are," we tell them and cannot decide if we're lying. Teaching English is crucial to advancing our country's geopolitical interests. I do not mean to make Bulgaria strange. But anything, I have discovered, is strange if depicted with apathetic precision. Stray dogs march through the streets as grizzly and stern as bureaucrats walking to work. A dumpster burns un-attended behind our apartment. On the sidewalk, I pass a man hugging a tree stump to his chest. On Sunday mornings M and I feed stray cats in the alleys. We make a point of naming the cats: Miffy, Zachary, Paris, Pickle, Chaz, Penelope, Meat Cat, and Cassandra. We have three human friends in our city. Two are a pair of musicians who met in America. Now, they bake, and we buy their bread every day. The third friend is Nikolai, a cheery ornithologist with bleached circles surrounding his eyes. He cashiers at a health food store owned by his wife. On rainy days he and I sit in the store discussing conspiracy theories, and I feel like a teenager, laughing, irreverent, confident in our shared paranoia. As a boy I was fat and friendship (meaning being invited to things) was my compensation for incessant derision. I was a paranoid child and have carried that feeling, cumbersome as a sack full of legs, into adulthood. M and I do not know who to trust. When we meet with the other 24 teachers we become frothy inside, longing to unburden ourselves, to cry, to complain, to snuggle inside of their ears—but we leave these meeting frightened we've told them too much. "When were you married?" one of them asks, corralling us as we exit a mixer. Even English requires translation. What she means is "Did you marry just for the visa?" We tell her we have somewhere to be. The secrets of others are currency here; they are traded for future promotions. We hear there are Mormons living in our city and spend weeks try-ing to find them. We cross paths in a park. They keep checking their watches, tapping their feet, glancing away as we chat. They say: "It was a pleasure to meet you." We say: "You don't need to go, do you?" They say: "We are really quite busy." We say: "Let's meet up again?" "Maybe," they say, and then scram. Both of us secretly fear—though we cannot admit this to each other—that we will end this trip with only each other as friends. But isn't that the point of a marriage? To need each other so fully we need no one else? Woodfire smoke thickens our city at night. The smoke is toxic but pleasant, seeps inside through our windows. I ride on a bus so hot that the driver is forced to pull over to the side of the highway. He opens the door. An elderly woman races up front and thrusts her head outside, joyously gasping. We drive the rest of the way with the door open. The air is the best I've felt in my life. It relaxes me as I ride to a doctor in Sofia. *Za'mnogo godini*. No. We do not fear we will die in this country—we fear only one of us will. *Za'mnogo godini*. As a precaution, we are rarely apart. M reaches for me in her sleep but our bed is too small for two people. I lie on the couch watching fire-works claw through a buttery fog.

TONY HOAGLAND

Achilles

Achilles is being carried from the field.
Three-fourths covered by a thin green gown; one big
bare shoulder sticking out; his face ash-gray and ivory-pale.
His war is finished. They're taking him home.

They have him in the bay across from me
on a gurney outside Radiology. IV bags suspended over his head
like toy Mylar balloons fastened to his arms by string.
Anyone can see he's done.

It seems we are temporarily encamped
on the bank of that famous river that has run
through London and Detroit, Bangkok and Bagdad—
this Ganges down which a hundred million souls have gone
like candles flickering in mist.

Our brave companions here: the corn-rowed orderly from Birmingham;
the plump Filipina nurse; Myron who spends his check on Powerball;
the weeping relatives. They move among us whispering.

Achilles—his name is called at last—
is being wheeled now on his way
into the crypt-cold vault called Radiology.

They roll him past. Maybe I am the only one
who sees the six tall ghosts that walk on either side of him,
rhythmically striking their fists against their shields.
I want to say, *Look, don't pity him! His imagination is not dead!*

Sideways, going by, he opens one of his gray eyes
to look at me, and raises two fingers in that salute
I am coming to recognize.

And then I am alone here,
the one to weep, and it is myself I weep for.

Inexhaustible Resource

"After the ocean rises, all this will be underwater,"
the biologist was saying, spreading her hands in the café,

"by which I mean," she clarified, "scuba diving in Manhattan:
floating past the stone gargoyles on the Chrysler Building,
swimming in and out the windows of Trump Tower."

No reason to get upset, says the Buddhist at the table;
Even the expression "global warming" is a case
                                        of planetary-centrism.

                    •

Carnage of the elephants and whales
Pandemic of the insects and the frogs
Scourge of the coral reefs and glaciers
Pillage of the rivers and of lakes
Eradication of crickets in the swamp, the fog hanging in the arms of coastal cypresses.

                    •

As John Keats, in his last letter, wrote,
"I have a feeling of my real life being past,
                and that I already am living my posthumous existence."

                    •

Even in these days before the coming storm,
our anguish, our handwringing and laments,
our statistical reports and scientific fights,

—can someone tell me, please
why they feel like a performance?

•

Imagination, our last system of immunity.
Disbelief, our most inexhaustible resource.
Unreality, my great love, protect me.

KEITH KOPKA

Etymology

I've been thinking we need a German word
for when someone you love,
or a celebrity, turns out to be
a scientologist.
       And I know the Germans
have already given us a word for the desire
one feels climbing through a window
to have sex with their first girlfriend
while her father, a floor below, sharpens
his ceremonial Prussian sword,

and another to describe the embarrassment
we feel on our own behalf when our friends'
dance moves look like their most sensitive
body parts have been hooked to a car battery,
while an orthodox priest revs the engine.

But the word I propose is more intricate,
acknowledges the choices we make,
while still capturing
the post coital pleasure that comes
when releasing small whiffs of judgment,
those justifying blankies we cuddle with
to sleep at night.

          Like when you're driving
and a squirrel darts at your car, so you break hard
just as it turns back to the shoulder,
and you think, *yeah buddy*! *Good call!*
But as you speed up again, the contents shift
in the tiny suitcase of its brain, and it turns
and jumps right under your tire.

The meaning of our word is not in this moment,
but, rather, in what comes after
when you start to admit to yourself that you
might have seen the squirrel starting to turn,
but you couldn't be bothered to break again,

how you feel sad for a second, but then think
you didn't invent the order of species,
and how at this point in history the damn thing
is designed absolutely to die.

But then again it's unclear whether you're upset
about killing something, or because you've
been trying to find parking for like twenty minutes,

and now that you finally have,
you're standing at the meter, and it keeps eating
your money without giving you back any time.

JESSICA GUZMAN ALDERMAN

Woman Unwittingly Joins Search Party Looking for Her

All day in the bus window, her face reflected
the misted chasm—a sweat-marked jaw—
so she swapped windbreaker and wool slacks
at the service stop. The driver's miscount,
the passengers whispered descriptors
—160cm, black shawl—crescendoed
across the canyon. I like to think I'd know
quickly, match myself first against
the inevitable call. Is it fabricate
or reconstruct when we daydream
ourselves into others? Three days from death
my father moaned a sound like my name
and pulled out his feeding tube, hands steady above
the obsidian mouth where I leaned my ear.

CYNTHIA HOGUE

The Underground Village

There was a village nearby in which everyone herded into the church feared the worst of course they did when an enemy officer was killed but regardless they obeyed as bewildered civilians what else could they do, one bad boy running off and in this way word got out of the church's great doors being barred from outside, the windows too high up to reach, the boy plugging his ears with tears having to hear them and remain hidden and they who bolted the doors, ordered to rough the people in, listened to all they'd wrought until silence fell, charred beams collapsing when tanks shoved walls in. For the rest of the war no one mentioned the neighboring village that had subtracted—disappeared—itself from a ground surface no longer shimmering greenly with safety for one, obeying without questions, but not the other, unasked. Now *not* them. Not soundly. The unheard screams entered their neighbors' dreams, resonants borne by wind, and so, into the vast maze of limestone caves beneath the fields muffling the lowing of the cows corralled below, the singular bark of goats. Above, in the inscrutable farmhouses, old women stirred stone soup in pots over fires they banked, baking an ashen bread. Murderers would arrive by supper.

MICHAEL BAZZETT

Lazarus

after Elizabeth Jennings

When Lazarus walked from the grave,
he tottered like a child letting go of a table
heading into the open for the first time.

His muscles were weak. Due to being dead,
I suppose. He was pale and waxy as a grub,
another drained thing out of the heavy

darkness. The smell confirmed it. Scent
cannot lie, it seems, and though this had
been the object of his mother's prayers,

when she hugged him and let the focus
of his eyes settle upon her like melting ice,
there was no doubt that part of what her

convoluted expression was grappling with
was the smell of meat gone round the bend.
Later, when he had bathed and dressed

in a clean robe she thought she'd folded
for the last time, she could still smell it,
a slight rank sweetness, like an orchid

in its final days, feeding its bloom with
one white toe in the dark earth. Only
this was decay delayed. This was birth.

GENEVIEVE KAPLAN

The history of that mine

Which was termed "abandonment," which was boarded
from outside, which was deemed "unsafe," an "attractive
nuisance," so I borrowed from it. Tiny items: a nail, a peg
a specially shaped gravel, a moment borne along and floating in
the image of an opening. Slant front and keyed along the edges
waiting, a small desired instance up the hill, in the sun—
we wanted shade but couldn't enter into its mouth. The dirt
inside differed so basically from the dirt outside. From rocks and dying
things. For inside: hope. And inside: depth. And maybe one part
that would glitter. A small piece that would catch. A little thing
and a worn thing and the moment to kindle a fire. Everyone gathered
upon the hill, around the edge, and tried their way very hardest
to look inside, and we all wished we could be there, too
for the moment one was carried out, dusty, on (and gleaming?) on
the back of (and bloody?) a mule.

VIET DINH

The Food Chain

THE LITTLE GIRL, HER FACE veiled in dust, hair bedraggled, emerges from the desert clutching a headless doll. The treads of her shoes are worn smooth by miles of hot highway. This stretch of land is frequented by families craving exposure to the splendor of America: mesas, rock formations carved by wind, the history of the earth in exposed geological strata, but the little girl knows only the road, a line in the desert that vanishes in distance, swallowed by watery heat mirages. She's lucky that a patrol car passes by, and as the officers drive her back towards Yucca City, twenty miles away, she slumps in the back seat, clasping the doll to her chest as if it were a weapon to defend against the desert encroaching on her clothes, her throat, her eyes. She doesn't answer the officers' questions, not even the simplest ones: her name, her parents' location, what she was doing wandering by herself. And it's not until they're halfway to the destination that she speaks, right as the car pulls by a dead Joshua tree, its bark withered and bleached tan, the branches, spindly and splintered, upright as if in prayer, and the little girl screams: "Mantis!"

•

THE HIGHWAY PATROL brings her to the Yucca City Community Health Clinic. NURSE MARTHA CORDINER offers her diagnosis: dehydration, shock, hysteric aphonia. Dr. Kaufman wanted to administer curare for the girl's muscle spasms, but she reminded him, *She probably only eight years-old.* She should have been a doctor, she thinks. She's just as smart as Dr. Kaufman, works twice as hard, and has never shown up to work plastered. This girl isn't the worst thing she's ever seen—that'd be the convertible full of teenagers crushed at 80 m.p.h.—but definitely the oddest. Occasionally, a Paiute wanders off the reservation, drunk as a skunk, and gets himself lost, but never a white girl. Sheriff Worley wants to know when the girl will be able to answer questions, and Martha replies, *However long it takes for her mind to recover.* If Martha were ten years younger, he'd be the type of man she'd run off with. He takes off his hat and runs a hand through his brown, curly hair. OK, twenty years younger. If it weren't for her husband Bob, she'd leave Yucca City. She has forty dollars and seven cigarettes in her purse—won't get far on either. She goes outside for a smoke. Leaning against the building, she pretends to be Jean Harlow—sultry, radiant. The glow of Las Vegas calls to her; further on, Hollywood. There's no place that doesn't need a nurse. That's how she'll start: a nurse. At first only in the background, a warm body in the hospital corridor scene, but then she'll get a line because she's the only one who can pronounce medical terminology: *diuretic, anterior, aqueous.* Then a few more lines. And then Gregory Peck falls in love with her because of her moxie and verve and her willingness to help little girls. Martha closes her eyes for the camera to pull in on her and Gregory's faces, and the breeze picks up, and there's a strange scratching noise behind her, but she's waiting for the close-up, the caress, the kiss.

•

THE NURSE WAS just here, DEPUTY NATHAN JOHNSON could swear it. She was just talking to the sheriff, but Deputy Johnson looks up and down the corridors of the clinic and there's no sign of her. The little girl sits alone, the left side of her face twitching. Children are the worst part of his job. Playing war with daddy's loaded gun, bespoiled by men with kind smiles, chewed up by the coyotes of the world. He, himself, was an orphan at 14. His father shot himself, his mother pickled herself with cooking sherry. *What were you doing out there?* he asks the girl. *By yourself?* From the window, the desert spreads out like a cheap beige blanket, both suffocatingly hot and not warm enough when you really need it. The cruelty of the world never lessens. He'd been saved from France, Germany, and those miniscule Pacific islands by the police academy, and he wishes he could be more grateful, but too many people have gone missing. That's a lot of children left on their own. Something white blows across the landscape like a tumbleweed. A nurse's cap. He radios the sheriff. He's got a tingling sensation at the base of his spine, like when his father pulled him aside and said, *You've got to take care of your Ma now, you hear?* He was eleven. The ranch where they lived was failing; the owner, a Californian carpetbagger, had never even set foot on the property. Steer auctioned for pennies on the pound. The military was going to turn the land into a proving ground. He tells the little girl, *You've got to take care of yourself, you hear?* His walkie-talkie crackles: *Johnson, we're right outside. You need to take a look at this.* He strokes her hair, whispers to her, *You're the only one who can.* When Johnson pokes his head out, he makes out a massive shape on the roof, black against the sun. The sheriff and DEPUTY JONATHAN RICHARDS draw their guns, aiming up. The shape lunges, catches him, and pinions him to the ground. The sheriff runs back inside, right past him. Richards is yanked into the air, and Johnson hears a grinding sound that reminds him of his hungry years, when he gnawed chicken bones to get at the marrow.

•

Two soldiers bring FRED CRANSTON into the basement of the hospital, where the rest of the staff has evacuated. He'd come in for a check-up on his gout, and the next thing he knows, he's jostled around. His left leg, from the thigh down, is gone. He should be in terrible pain but feels light-headed, pleasantly woozy. Nurse Mayer attends the other patients, and Sheriff Worley holds a little girl in his arms. The walls are concrete, and the battle outside rains down with percussive force: gunfire, snare drums; heavy artillery, a timpani. *Dulce et decorum est*, Cranston thinks. He imagines Ryan, his son, bleeding out in Okinawa, jabbed in the abdomen by a spear, a wound which, had a doctor been there, would have been cleaned out and stitched up without a problem. But instead: mud, sepsis, seizures. How many comrades passed Ryan by, how many stepped on him, how many fell by his side? There is no good way to die, not during war. Around him, in the dusty basement, he sees, on everyone's face, his own the day the Western Union messenger came around: THE SECRETARY OF WAR DESIRES ME TO EXPRESS HIS DEEP REGRET… Dr. Kaufman asks, *What have you been drinking?* God, what *hasn't* he been drinking? The alcohol sublimating from his pores fills the room with the smell of antiseptic. Upstairs, a clamor. The sheriff puts his hand on the gun. The creature, whatever it is, is too large to come down the stairs. This basement is a designated civil defense shelter. They have food and water. They can wait it out. It's what he's done since Ryan died. Wait. Everyone needs a shelter, he thinks, a safe place. War follows him even now. It always invades any safe place he finds. He looks at his leg, a jagged, raw severing. There is no escape. He won't survive the hour. But Dr. Kaufman unbuckles his belt for a makeshift tourniquet. *Let's staunch the bleeding*, he says. That's something, at least.

•

Through his scope, SPECIALIST ALAN GREEN can see almost everything. The ground unit, hunkered behind their vehicles, keeps the creature trapped on the roof. From his vantage point on a nearby bluff, he has a clear shot. People are amazed by snipers—*Your aim must be astounding*, they say—but it's not the aim. It's the math. Bullet velocity, target distance, wind resistance. The numbers fall into place before he pulls the trigger. The pinwheel gauge next to him registers nothing, so he won't have to wind dope. Hollow point in the barrel for a better ballistic coefficient and down-range velocity retention. In his crosshairs, he's got the creature's eye, a nice round target. He's a go. He braces his feet in the dirt, rests the rifle on his shoulder, takes a deep breath, holds it. The weight is comfortable. He resists the urge to blink. And—*contact*. The creature shakes its head, staggered. It wobbles on spindly legs. The bullet, by now, has mushroomed inside the eye, obliterating it. Maybe penetrated to the brain. He smells freshly-burnt powder. His right clavicle stings from the kick.

He'll have to adjust the butt on his next go. But it doesn't look like there'll be next time. The creature falls off the roof, and the troops scatter, but when it's clear that it's not getting up, they cheer. Their arms rise, and they clap each other on the back. It takes a few seconds for the sound to reach him. Back at base, there'll be a celebration tonight. The wind gauge picks up. A breeze brushes by with the sound of helicopter rotors, different from any Hoverflies he's heard. Dark specks in the sky. He focuses in with binoculars and sees a black cloud of those creatures, flying towards the clinic. More than he has bullets for, more than he can count. The guys on the ground don't know what's coming. He calls out, but the math is not in his favor. Velocity, distance, resistance: his voice is not a bullet. He tries to hail someone on the radio, he waves his arms, and, through his binoculars again, he sees one soldier pointing right at him, at the shadow that's suddenly come up behind him.

•

BULLETS RICOCHET OFF their chitin; grenades cracks it, but don't break it. They have two weak points: the eyes, and the shoulder joints of their main arms. A good hit means they're blind or that they topple over, immobile, but the fact that the damn things *fly* makes it more difficult. But as long as they have a vulnerability, they can die, SERGEANT GORDON thinks. He has to keep them in one place on the ground and hit them while they're eating, but no one in his right mind volunteers for munch duty. He trained these boys; during boot camp, he went hoarse disciplining them, honing them. They're *his* boys, a fighting force, a metal fist. He's ordered one group to round up cattle. The ranchers don't like the requisitioning of their herds, but this is a national emergency. They corral the steers in a circle and take positions in fortified trenches. He says: *Stay frosty, boys.* Maybe the high muckity-mucks have another plan—they *so* love to strategize—but he can't wait. Not after what happened to the squad at Yucca City. As night falls, the heat drops to nothing, and they shine klieg lights on the cattle. The cow breaths are visible as they snort; they sleep standing up. His boys do the same, half-asleep on watch. He jolts 'em awake: ears open, eyes up front. What are you: soldiers or Boy Scouts? They shiver in their boots, fingers crystallizing around triggers, but this makes him feel alive. Then, the thrumming sound, like a low roll of thunder. *Come and get it*, he mutters. The things land, turn their heads as if looking around, and chow down. *Wait, wait*, he whispers, and once the cows are half-gone—man, the things eat like slobs—he orders, *Now now now!* Muzzle flashes, dull thuds as slugs hit shells, tiny metallic tings as grenade pins are pulled and the spring engages. *Come on, boys*, he calls, *light 'em up!* Clods of dirt fly in the air. He counts five of the things, twitching and flinching, as if in pain. Sergeant Gordon feels like a proud poppa. But—he sees it happen, as if in slow-motion—one bug deflects a live grenade off its leg, a lucky, one-in-a-million hit, and it flies back into the trench. The sergeant reacts, throwing himself onto it, a cold lump pressing into his stomach. He thinks of them, his boys.

•

DR. HELMUT KRASNER has waited for this. The life of an entomologist is a lonely one. When he announces that he's being flown to Nevada for a *top-secret military* consultation, his children don't react. His son keeps a pack of cigarettes in his rolled-up shirt sleeve, a defiant bicep, while his daughter wears poodle skirts that lose an inch of hem with every wash. Dr. Krasner works through the night, fueled by coffee and nips of scotch, until his esophagus burns and fingers buzz. Beth comes in at midnight, giggling, and Colin even later, silent and grim. No one takes him seriously. The university has drained funds from zoology for medicine, atomic physics, and robotics. Robots! No robot could have formulated such an elegant answer to the mantid problem: guaranteed success with no human casualties, a solution so simple that only a genius could see it. When the military Jeep picks him up, his son mouths the word *pig*. In the Stratoliner, cruising above the country, his chest tightens. The altitude makes him dizzy. Entomology is just as important now as when Hans Hermann Behr collected his first Lepidoptera. Krasner is the foremost expert on *Stagmomantis Carolina*, and if they don't listen to him, who will they listen to? Stanley Frimlet? The hack who wants to order mantids in Dictyoptera? He slows his panting, shakes away his mental fuzz. If what he's read in the briefing is true, then this is a new species. Once he's examined and described it, he will name it. Soldiers salute as he steps off the plane. In the wood-lined operations room, the chiefs-of-staff gather around a heavy mahogany table, old men with faces square from hair to jaw. The pressure in his chest builds again, and he thinks, *Mantis gigantibet*, for his daughter. The heat spreads into his body, veins throbbing, and he manages to say, *Gentleman, the solution is very simple, very final*, before he clutches his chest. As he collapses, he thinks, *Mantis giganticol*, for his son, Colin, who would appreciate the joke and might, one day, respect his father for it.

•

WELL, THE FIRST egghead was a wash, but SPC. MARCUS GORDON prefers the second one. The non-dead one. There, at Command & Control HQ on the Proving Grounds, 30 miles from Yucca City, Egghead #2 lays out a nightmare scenario: one egg case cluster can contain up to 300 mantid young. His map shows red arrows radiating out of Nevada like a spider, into California, into Utah, across the country. *Great!* thinks Gordon. He's hitched his wagon to Gen. McLaughlin, and if Eisenhower rode WWII right into the White House, then he can ride Gen. McLaughlin's coattails up the ranks. The general thinks big and bold: compulsory military service for all males 18-25; mandatory volunteerism for the war effort; overnight shifts at munitions factories; expansion of the ground observer corps. They could commandeer the airwaves to boost patriotism everywhere. People are afraid, and they should be! War isn't for the meek. Right now, battle options are limited: regular bullets didn't do much, but in the air, A-4 Skyhawks can blitz their wings into lace doilies, and, on the ground, flamethrower crews can come in for a barbeque. They've kept the threat contained, but in a few days, a few hours—who knows? The President demands status reports every twenty minutes. Gordon mans the board, an etched-glass map in the middle of the room; on it, he marks vectors of aircraft and hostiles alike. Here's the plan: two hundred miles away, at Nellis AFB, B-66 Destroyers are queued up with a special payload recommended by Egghead #2. Ground troops have been ordered to hold the line. Unless the bugs are completely localized, this strategy will fail. Egghead #2 was particularly alarmist: *This could be the end of humanity as the top of the food chain!* Gen. McLaughlin has Nellis AFB on the line when the chunk of ceiling comes down, shattering the map. A bug leg pokes its way through the hole. Gen. McLaughlin yells, *Deploy!* Men scatter to the sides of the room; those near windows are speared and pulled out. As the building comes down, Spc. Gordon turns to say, *Sir, it's been an honor serving with you*—but Gen McLaughlin has already fled. The skittering grows louder. *Well, dammit*, Gordon thinks.

•

PVT. DANIELS PRESSES against the trench, smelling earth, sage roots, blood. If he stays very still, the mantis' compound eyes won't detect him, and he might not get skewered. The survivors listen for the beating of wings, the clicking of mandibles. Occasionally, a mantis leg darts into the trench, a sliver of green lightning, and an unlucky soldier snags his uniform—or his flesh—on a spine and gets hoisted out. The screams don't go on *too* long, but any length of time is bad enough. He's known some of those guys since boot camp. But they have their orders, straight from the mouth of Gen. McLaughlin, and he knows that, as a grunt, he's cannon fodder. Though, he always thought he'd go against the Communists, or the Fourth Reich, or the Communists of the Fourth Reich. The shadows deep in the trench lighten, and he relaxes because the main feeding time is ending. He wants to slither on his belly all the way back to Arkansas. But his orders are to hold this ground, so he pushes himself further into the dirt wall, surprisingly moist for a desert. He wraps his arms around his legs and rests his head on his knees, as if doubled-over in prayer, and, from above, hears a drone. Not mantis wings, but something more soothing: propellers. Air support! At long last! He climbs out of the trench to watch the planes, a squadron, and as they pass overhead, he takes off his helmet and waves, cheers them on. They drop something from their cargo holds. Not bombs—there's no whistling sound. Parachutes billow from the payloads. They look like dogwood blooms. Midway down, they pop, and long purple tendrils extend from each package, a fireworks display. The sky turns lavender. He watches it fall on him like dusk. It burns to the touch, and he jumps back down in the trench, where the rest of the men gag, coughing, scratching their chests. Pvt. Daniels looks for his gas mask, but his eyes water too much, he can't see, and his throat feels as if he's been drinking gasoline and just swallowed a lit match.

•

AT THE 20TH year memorial service for the Mantid War, Grace Johnson, the first witness and the first survivor of known Mantid attacks, now a young woman, speaks. Her speech has been prepared and vetted by the Department of Defense, and spotlights that had once been trained on the horizon to illuminate the chitinous bodies of advancing mantids now train on her. Draped behind her, on-stage, is an enormous American flag, supposedly the same flag that flew above the Yucca City Community Health Clinic, though it's too big to be true. She speaks with strength and purpose, the way she's rehearsed. Most of the country was never touched by the war, not the way she was, not the way Nevada was, and there might have been a few over-publicized abuses of martial law (accidental shootings of protesting seditionists, detainees with lost paperwork who therefore couldn't be released), but are they safer now than 20 years ago? Yes. Yes, they are. She is, she says, the embodiment of co-operation between the civilian and the military. It was a Yucca City policeman who had rescued her, and it was a family in Arkansas who, having lost their son in the war, adopted her. Pvt. Daniels, she reads, will always be my brother—and here, she pauses and sputters—but only for a moment, short enough that her military handlers don't notice, and concludes her speech. Later, back in her hotel (she's flown in from the mantid-free East Coast, though lately there have been reports of tarantulas the size of watermelons, thanks to the Zyklops-4 that turned the tide of battle), she thinks about her brother, ALEX, on the day he died. Not at the moment of his death—that memory is still lost in the haze of her sub-conscious—but on the morning of. Her parents, JOHN and SALLY, were packing the car, and her brother had cornered her against the porch railing of the motel. A then-normal-sized praying mantis perched on his index finger, and he held it to her face as she squirmed and whined because she knew he wanted her to be scared, and that by acting scared, she'd get him in trouble and receive a pre-lunch cookie as consolation, and she could not stop looking at it, the way it turned its head, as if it were as curious about her as she was of it. *It's coming for you, Gracie*, Alex said. *You'd better watch out.*

Translation Folio

GABRIELA MISTRAL

Translators' Introduction

Velma García-Gorena & Kate Berson

GABRIELA MISTRAL (1889-1957), BORN Lucila Godoy Alcayaga, was a Chilean poet, essayist, schoolteacher, diplomat, and activist for the rights of women, children, and indigenous peoples. The first Latin American to win the Nobel Prize in literature (1945), she remains the only female Nobel laureate in the Spanish language.

Mistral was born in the village of Montegrande to a family of modest means. During her adolescence, she worked as a rural schoolteacher to support her family and began publishing her poetry in regional newspapers. By the 1920s, she was well-known throughout the Spanish-speaking world, both for her poetry and her support of rural education. In 1922, the new revolutionary Mexican government invited her to Mexico to establish the country's rural school system. There, she met revolutionary scholars and artists such as José Vasconcelos, Alfonso Reyes, Diego Rivera, and Frida Kahlo, whose work emphasized the indigenous side of Mexican culture. Subsequently, Mistral would identify as *mestiza*—of Spanish as well as indigenous ancestry—and would focus on the plight of indigenous people in her writing. In addition to poetry, Mistral wrote numerous essays on human rights, international politics, and world peace. In 1925, she joined the Chilean diplomatic corps and worked in Europe, Brazil, and Mexico. In the 1930s, she taught at Barnard, Vassar, and Middlebury Colleges. After winning the Nobel Prize, she lived in Mexico, Italy, and New York, where she served as a member of the Chilean consulate.

Gabriela Mistral's work reflects her experience abroad and the perspective she gained as a result. She wrote about Latin American identity, using regional language while extolling the indigenous populations of the Americas. She also explored the world of mothers and children, especially in her first book of poetry, *Desolación* (1922). For many years, critics viewed her poetry as conservative: the poet glorified the maternal role and seemed to be advocating that women should stay in the domestic sphere. However, more recent feminist criticism has emphasized Mistral's often veiled subversive view of maternity and gender roles.[1]

Desolación was a great critical success (Mistral's only book translated into English and published in its entirety), as were her subsequent works, *Ternura* (Tenderness) and *Tala* (Harvest) published in 1924 and 1938. Mistral was awarded the Nobel Prize in

---

1. Karen Peña, *Poetry and the Realm of the Public Intellectual* (London: Legenda, 2007), 33.

1945 "for her lyric poetry which, inspired by powerful emotions, has made her name a symbol of the idealistic aspirations of the entire Latin American world."[2]

Mistral's last two books, *Lagar* (Winepress, 1956) and *Poema de Chile* (1967), no longer focus on motherhood but rather reflect Mistral's shifting interests and concerns as a mature woman who has experienced numerous tragedies, including the suicide of her son and the deaths of her mother and sister. Other poems refer to the tragedy of war, and the exile that follows - once again, a reflection of Mistral's experience. Mistral lived in Europe at the time of the Spanish Civil War and World War II, which led her to become a pacifist and human rights activist.

A common perspective on Mistral's work has centered on the poet's personal life: she purportedly was a sad, saintly Catholic spinster, longing for a husband and children. But this interpretation is now being challenged by the emergence of a large collection of her papers and audio recordings that were made public eight years ago. When Mistral died in Hempstead, Long Island in 1957, she left all her papers and possessions to her partner and executor, Doris Dana, who only allowed limited access to a few scholars. When Dana died in 2006 and named her niece, Doris Atkinson, as executor, Atkinson inherited two tons of materials belonging to Mistral, including 10,000 pages of correspondence, unpublished poetry, drafts of published poems, and almost fifty hours of recordings of Mistral's life with Doris Dana and their friends. Atkinson donated everything to the Biblioteca Nacional de Chile (Chile's national library) with the stipulation that all of the papers should be made public and put online.

These materials have led to a re-interpretation of the poet's life and work. Mistral was not a lonely spinster. She had a romantic partner, Dana, many close friends, and an adoptive son. She practiced a liberal version of Catholicism combined with Buddhism, theosophy, and Judaism. These newly discovered materials have renewed scholarly and public interest in Mistral's life and work, and have led to the publication of ten books, as well as a documentary, "Locas Mujeres," by the Chilean documentary film-maker, María Elena Wood.

"Meeting the Deer" and "The Desert" are taken from Mistral's last book, *Poema de Chile*, which addresses entrenched, systemic social problems in Chile and Latin America. *Poema* was published posthumously and critics appear to have been hesitant to study a text some considered to be "unfinished." Nevertheless, Mistral considered *Poema* to be her superior and seminal work. It symbolized her love for Chile, as well as her appreciation of the countryside and Chile's indigenous population. In *Poema*, Mistral's ghost returns to Earth and walks through the Chilean countryside, from north to south, in the company of a young indigenous boy from the Atacama desert and a *huemul*, an Andean deer. The collection describes the beauty of the land, embraces

---

2. https://www.nobelprize.org/nobel_prizes/literature/laureates/1945/mistral-facts.html

social justice, and emphasizes the importance of protecting the countryside and its animal and human inhabitants.

Mistral's work insists that rural land provides this woman-spirit (the poet's ghost) and the Mapuche boy with refuge from society's ills and hierarchy. In many of the poems, the spirit carefully steers the boy and deer away from urban areas. In fact, during her own lifetime, Mistral suffered upon leaving her home village of Montegrande. In Santiago and other cities, upper class people mocked her for being from the "wrong" side of the tracks, for not having proper teaching credentials, and for her lack of traditional femininity.

Poema de Chile, a long text made up of individual poems written in a single meter, can be considered a national poem for its illumination and encapsulation of Chile's history, present moment, and future.[3] But unlike Pablo Neruda's epic poem, *Canto General, Poema de Chile* is not about a heroic man returning to his native land; instead, an un-heroic female spirit comes back to the countryside she loved in order to teach a young boy from a marginalized indigenous population about the injustice imposed by Spanish colonialism. *Poema* includes critiques of the race, class, and gender hierarchies still present in Chile, Latin America, and indeed around the world.

---

3. Eliabeth Horan, *Gabriela Mistral: An Artist and Her People* (Washington, D.C.: OAS, 1994), 184.

GABRIELA MISTRAL : Two Poems

Meeting the Deer

There I went, crisscrossing
thickets, deserts,
spotting clumps of cacti
and armies of ants
when your eyes jumped out at me,
when your whole body jumped out
from a tangle of ferns,
your neck and your dear body
in the light, like a young pine.

You were born in the oldest
land of the Incas, you, my deer,
where we begin,
and where they're disappearing;
and now you guide me
or it's me leading you.
How well you understand the soul
and remind me I have a body!

They're quite sad, my little one,
those friendless paths:
they feel like a long yawn
like a drunk stumble.
Don't take them, don't follow them
they may lead to your death.

Clever of you to choose instead
ravine, forest, and thicket.
When asked they will not answer
to the lost, nor the blind
and they are like Canidia
the witch who tries only to confound us.

But, yes, you understand
their slithering malice . . .

We walk together
like this, pretend siblings
you casting the shadow of a boy
while mine is but a fern . . .

(How wonderful for an Angel-deer
to appear amidst such solitude!)

Maybe it's because you're found
on the Chilean coin
and when you saw me you came,
and you lead me or I lead you
in the direction determined
by the tilt of your head.

People lose faith
in the paths
when doves scatter
or when the deer's neck stiffens and tilts
even though a fawn makes a better guide
than a deceitful human being.

Let's see if by walking, burning across
league after league, we'll finally learn
that the deer is born to navigate
these roads, paths, and danger.

You surely deserve to be lifted
above my former kingdom
to be shown the gods
who, out of mud and light, created you.
More than any man, you deserve
to run happy through the heavens
without getting caught in spiny thickets
or chased down paths,
you, Deer, guilty only
of contemplating the wind . . .

Turn around then, little fawn,
and don't make of yourself a companion
for this crazy woman,
confused and losing her way,
because she's forgotten everything
except one valley and one village.

This valley they call Elqui
and Montegrande, my heart's keeper.
Though I left, I can still feel it
in what they call the chest,
though I no longer have a name
nor cast a shadow walking
and the orchards cannot hear me pass
and no village can detect me.
How could they possibly see me,
those sleeping here in the hills,
and dream their marvelous dreams
my dead have told me about?
Soon I too will sleep
and have a dream of my own,
filled with peace,
much peace and forgetting,
there where I once lived,
where river and mountain made
my voice and my silence
and neither Coyote nor Coyota
neither bile nor ice I bore.

The Desert

Let's make a pact on the road
a pact between friends
because we're getting close
to the land of distress
to the crust now turning brown,
to the poor Grandfather Desert.

The God of green grass who made
the gardens of Tacna,
gave us too this pelt of desert;
and this skinless skull
and this crackling fire
were also my inheritance
and I will not deny them.

I've lived and died in deserts:
they were mine and they're mine now
and since I'm loyal, I will still
taste their salty sand.

No, don't look at the sand
nor the low, stubborn rocks.
Let's hope you sleep until
a stream appears,
hiss of water, shimmer
of running water I don't see.

Seems as if with every step
its burning hand will guide us.
Seems to be just it alone
with its partner, the wind.
Seems it will trick you
with its taunts, advice, or stories
but the desert's all about
gritted, chattering teeth,
a brine-filled throat

and everywhere the lick of fire.
Your tongue begs for water;
your only wish is for water
and as you lower yourself to the sand
this bonfire of a desert scorches you.
If I spy a stream
I'll quickly put you down.
The mist I offer you
and these short fresh breaths
are my very own vapor,
what's left of my body.

The earth, it gives you nothing,
my scared long-lashed fawn.
Let me carry you, bring you,
in my arms, little one.
Don't buck, don't break
the bit of body I still have;
don't roll around like that,
mischievous one,
see the dust you're getting
in your eyebrows, pelt, and neck.
Settle down once and for all, close
your eyes, summon sleep.

translated from the Spanish by Velma García-Gorena and Kate Berson

HASANTHIKA SIRISENA

Broken Arrow

> No movement and no breath, no progress nor mistakes,
> Nothing begins or ends, no one loves or fights,
> All your foes are friends and all your days are nights
> And all the roads lead round and are not roads at all

> —Louis MacNeice

1961

ON JANUARY 22, ALONG THE coast of North Carolina, the eight-man crew of a B-52 realizes their plane is losing fuel too fast. The right wing might be damaged but there's no way for them to check. Only two members of the crew can see outside, and all that is visible to either of them is the night sky and the ocean: a purple-red bruise intersecting at the horizon. The pilot, Major Tulloch, radios Seymour Johnson Air Force Base in Goldsboro that the plane must make an emergency landing. This wouldn't be particularly notable except that the *Keep-19* mission is part of the Strategic Air Command and is on a test run for a program meant to allow the United States to be the first to attack in case of a nuclear war. The plane carries two Mark 39 thermonuclear weapons, in other words two hydrogen bombs. Both of these bombs together have an explosive yield 500 times greater than the bomb that destroyed Hiroshima and a kill range of somewhere between seven and eight and a half miles. Each is active, ready to detonate upon being dropped.

The January night is cold and, because of a front moving through, the air at that altitude is estimated at 150 knots. (A Category 1 hurricane measures winds of 62 to 82 knots). During the second mid-air refueling the turbulence is so strong Tulloch struggles to keep the plane steady. He feels every buffet and pitch in his muscles, in his bones. The cockpit of the bomber is not a comfortable place. It is all metal and glass and smells of sweat, burnt rubber, and urine. The crew has been on alert, not just for the ten-hour flying time, but also before that on the ground as they waited hours to receive their commands. They are, by now, simultaneously tired and wired, fueled by adrenaline and raw desire to complete the mission. At some point during the refueling, the pilot reportedly asks a co-pilot to hand-fly the plane so he can rest a moment. It takes at least three tries to finish what should be a simple process.

Flying a plane takes strength, coordination, and mental stamina under any circumstances. B-52 Stratofortresses are massive planes; 200 tons of metal, a wingspan of over 180 feet, eight engines. In the sky, these are the hulking monsters of war movies, casting long shadows that slide menacingly across fields and mountains. On the runway, the bulk slows the bomber down and causes it to waddle as it accelerates. The standard instrument panel consists of eight throttles and thirty-two gauges for monitoring the engines.

But I am not being fair when I reconstruct this plane using only bolts and metal plates, tonnage and turbo-power. The B-52 is surprisingly sensitive with a delicately balanced central nervous system dedicated ultimately to maintaining life. I am always shocked when I read about plane crashes (as I like to do) to realize that planes aren't built to beat nature—nothing manmade can at an altitude of 40,000 feet—but to defy it, like an extended and especially precarious game of tiddlywinks.

Major Tulloch is a career soldier with the thick, beefy features of an extra in a World War II re-enactment. He enlisted after Pearl Harbor at the age of twenty-nine and has served ever since, first as a soldier and later as a fighter pilot and a test pilot. He has hundreds of hours of combat experience and has walked away from three test plane crashes. He is by military standards an 'old man' at forty-six and at least a decade and a half older than most of the crew. But he is the sort of man SAC wants flying these missions: seasoned, tough, capable.

He is not afraid when the crew reports that they have lost nineteen tons of fuel in little under two minutes. He does not imagine as I do some dumb, dinosaur–like beast, suspended high above, beyond our ken, bleeding out, slowly dying. He does not feel that frisson of excitement, that metallic taste on the tongue, at the thought of some great catastrophe. He is too professional to indulge imagination. He listens instead as the *Addle 57*, the fuel tanker, informs him they have spotted the leak at the base of the right wing. He knows he and his crew are in some danger though he does not know how much. He also understands that with that much fuel, with that much weight, they cannot land or the plane will break apart. They must stay aloft. He does as he is commanded: he moves the plane several hundred miles off the coast of Wilmington to prevent, if they do have to crash land, possible nuclear destruction.

1975

A FEW MONTHS into his first job in America, at Cherry Hospital in Goldsboro, North Carolina, my father is assigned Frank Washington, a paranoid schizophrenic who everyone else in his unit is afraid of. According to my father, Frank grew up in Brooklyn and served time in New York State for assaulting a man. When the state released

Frank from Sing Sing, the corrections officer gave him a bus ticket and told him to travel as far away as possible. Frank had made it to North Carolina before voices instructed him to stab a man in a bus terminal restroom. The day of his release from the North Carolina correctional facility, Frank refused to leave. The guards turned a high-pressure water hose on him to blast him from his cell and admitted him to Cherry Hospital because, as his court-appointed lawyer put it, "You had to be crazy not to want to leave jail."

Frank is a small man, lithe but powerful. He is African American. Unlike many of the other patients at Cherry Hospital who take little interest in their personal hygiene, he dresses in neatly kept, well-fitting clothes. The orderlies and nurses are afraid of Frank and refuse to get on an elevator alone with him, claiming he hides a shank somewhere on his body. Behind his back, they make fun of Frank's composure, call him queer.

According to my father, no one else wants to take Frank on as a patient, and he doesn't really have a choice either. I wonder, when my father tells me this, if he wasn't assigned Frank as some sort of punishment. My father, all his life, has elicited from others respect for his intelligence and confidence, and the desire to put him in his place. The latter he brings on himself. He is charming but also quick-tempered, often rude and abrasive with little warning.

During the patient interview, my father watches Frank closely. Frank is calm, almost listless, and he doesn't make eye contact. He is thirty-eight, making him and my father close to each other in age. But this man before my father is alone—with any family long ago lost to him—and very ill. He keeps his hands on the table in front of him where everyone can see them, another sign of life spent in institutions.

My father asks Frank if he knows what the following proverb means: a watched pot never boils. Frank takes a long time to respond. When he finally does, he speaks to the corner of the room. He explains that if you watch a pot the water won't boil. This isn't an indication of the man's intelligence but a symptom, instead, of his disease. He prefers, perhaps can only comprehend, the literal. His mind cannot contend with the deeper, figurative meaning.

My father notes the response on the patient's chart. When he looks back, he is distracted momentarily by some feeling of sorrow. He isn't supposed to be here, he thinks. He is here by accident. He's very well-prepared and very ambitious. He left Sri Lanka in the early 70s to complete a prestigious fellowship in England. He was supposed to arrive in a New World, but this world, rendered barren by the cool October wind, looks anything but new. The fields with their hardened dark earth and desiccated cornstalks are used and unpromising. Cherry Hospital feels worn and tired with its decades-old brick buildings. In movies, on television, American hospitals had looked bright, all white, with young and attractive nurses and doctors. Cherry Hospital reeks of ammonia and mildew.

Frank complains of pain in his arm and shoulder. Last week, my father and Frank had had a lively conversation about boxing. Both were boxers in their youth and they bonded over this shared interest. But Frank isn't lively today. This might be the pain; it might be the Haldol. Frank begins to explain that the pain is caused by radio waves, emitted by a transmitter at Seymour Johnson Air Force Base. This is a man whose brain has splintered, a brain that doesn't properly process sensory information. It doesn't process social cues. Frank's victim at the bus terminal may have taunted him or he may have smiled.

I learn all this during a series of interviews I conduct with my father for a novel that I never published. My father also explains to me that the lawyer was wrong. Frank wasn't 'crazy' for not wanting to leave jail. According to my father, mentally ill patients often seek the comfort and shelter of a rigorously structured environment. It eases the confusion and disorientation. My father speaks solemnly, his expression is one of compassion.

Frank is the only patient my father has *ever* spoken about to me. Frank stays with him and bothers him. He is one of the reasons that my father—who became certified to practice both psychiatry and general medicine—decided to leave psychiatry and build instead an internal medicine practice. I don't know why, out of the hundreds of patients my father treated in his forty-year career, Frank stays with him. He does reveal Frank's complete diagnosis: paranoid schizophrenia due to socio-cultural deprivation.

"We thought it was a joke," my father says to me. By we he means his colleagues at the hospital, many who were immigrants as well. "The diagnoses we were making. Socio-cultural deprivation! We'd never heard of that diagnosis in England."

I didn't really understand what this might have meant to my father until recently. I was trying to explain to my new boss, a South African who immigrated to the States in his twenties, what it was like to grow up in the South. I mentioned my father's anger about the diagnoses. My boss cocked his head and thought about this for a moment. Then he added, "That must have been something for your father, coming from where he did."

I shook my head not understanding. My boss smiled gently. "Your father thinks he's coming to the first world, to modernization. Instead he finds socio-cultural deprivation." When I still didn't quite get it, my boss added, "Your father replaced one third world experience for another."

The Crash

SOMEWHERE CLOSE TO midnight, the Keep-19 crew is told to return to Seymour John-son Air Force Base. No one truly knows the extent of the structural damage to the wing, but another B-52 in a similar situation had landed safely. They are landing in Goldsboro, not out at sea, because the military does not want to lose their expensive payload to the ocean. Two hydrogen bombs are not an easy loss to explain and the operations are only in their testing phases. That these military strategists did not quan-tify or identify the extraordinary destruction that would take place if one of those bombs detonated over Goldsboro, North Carolina is profoundly disturbing. These are the same men who can imagine, quantify, extrapolate, demonstrate the massive loss of life and destruction that would take place if Russia dropped a bomb on us. They seem not to understand that, at this moment, the biggest threat comes from within.

Air traffic control clears the *Keep-19* mission crew to land at Seymour Johnson Air Force Base. They wish the crew luck, an acknowledgement that everyone on the ground understands the plane is in danger. The crew is able to lower the landing gear and the wing flaps without incident. Major Tulloch positions them to land. But, the plane continues to turn on its own. The copilots stomp the rudder pedals, pull the control wheel hard left. Their muscles twitch and pop with the effort. The acid burn of near exhaustion floods their bodies but they have trained themselves not to give in. These efforts aren't enough. The plane barrel rolls. The crew hears and feels the ex-plosion, then realizes the right wing has snapped off. What starts as a crack becomes, through the forces of physics and nature, a splintering and then a shattering as if 200 tons of steel and wire is nothing more than a plate being knocked from a table or a mirror loosened from its wall mount.

Major Tulloch gives the command to the crew to bail. Their response is not the terror-stricken, catastrophic hysteria depicted in movie plane crashes. They are trained for this and remain calm. One crewmember asks Tulloch to repeat his command be-cause he isn't sure he's heard correctly. "Bail out," Tulloch insists with more urgency. Only six of the eight crew members can use ejector seats. The 'extras' must make their way to an escape hatch on the lower level in the belly of the plane. A copilot, Lieutenant Adam Mattocks, removes his headset and unbuckles his seatbelt. When he tries to stand, the g-force slams him backward with such force that he blacks out. When he recovers consciousness, he sees Tulloch struggling violently, and vainly, to maintain control of the plane as it descends.

Mattocks realizes he cannot make it to the lower level and that he is most likely going to die. He attempts a maneuver no one has survived: he bails, without an ejec-tor seat, from an open over-head hatch. He's lucky—very lucky. Because the plane is spinning, the overhead hatch is no longer overhead but instead positioned to the left.

He doesn't fall onto the plane or any of its wreckage but free of it. He describes a moment of inertia—of being suspended. It must have been beautiful in its awfulness. This plane spiraling as Mattocks somersaults in tandem: metal and flesh silhouetted against a perfect, yellow pinhole moon.

A Roll of the Dice

IN THE PAST few years, we've spoken so much about Goldsboro that I can easily imagine life for my father back then. I can invoke my father as he finishes his breakfast—sardines on toast and a cup of milk tea. I can hear the sirens wail. Many of the employees of Cherry Hospital live in housing provided by the hospital. The siren—heard across the campus—marks the change from the evening shift to the morning.

He swipes the corners of his mouth with a napkin, stands and makes his way from the dining room to the front door where his coat—his favorite tweed blazer that he bought from Marks & Spencer in London—is hanging. He passes me seated on the floor, cross-legged, eating a bowl of cereal and watching the *Uncle Paul Show*. A grown man in a top hat marches a gaggle of children in a circle in time to some inane children's song. I am riveted, absolutely enthralled and do not register my father's presence in the room. When, he wonders, have they begun allowing me to eat breakfast in front of the television? He hears my mother in the bedroom getting dressed so that she can walk me to school. The idea overwhelms him that he is making some sort of mistake. He has brought his family into a world which despite his considerable intelligence, he cannot decode or comprehend, and when he tries to sleep at night his mind somersaults envisioning failure after failure.

He claimed, many times during my childhood, he really wanted a job in New Zealand. The hospital was interested and New Zealand and Australia heavily recruited doctors like my father. In his re-telling he doesn't get the New Zealand job because his boss in London decided not to mail his recommendation. My father didn't want to return to Sri Lanka because of the political turmoil and because he felt there was little opportunity for him there. My father accepted the post at Cherry Hospital after interviewing for the position in London, and he took the job without visiting the hospital or North Carolina before arriving.

My father confessed recently that if he'd known what North Carolina was going to be like he wouldn't have come. I asked him why he decided to stay then. At first, when things were the worst, he didn't have the money to return. Later, he didn't want to wrench us, his daughters, from the home we knew. Eventually, he came to like his patients, and he thought he was serving them in some way. "But I wouldn't have believed that at first," he admitted. "For a long time, I knew I had made a mistake."

I am not trying to compare my father's immigration—which was, in fact a success—to a plane crash. Perhaps it's my age or where I am in my life, but I am fascinated by the calculations we make, the line between triumph and failure. What I know about probability I know from dad who loved mathematics, and studied it, as a hobby, all his life. And what I know is that the study of probability, statistics, is the study, ultimately, of how we think and reason. The mathematician Pierre-Simon Laplace marks induction—drawing a particular conclusion from many outcomes—as a major moment of progress in science, math, morality, and justice. As he notes in his *Philosophical Essays on Probability*, we are afraid of the comet the first time we see it, believe it is the cause of the fall of an empire. By the fourth revolution, though, we have come to understand the laws of nature and we understand that our comet is not at all connected to our fate. He also acknowledges that if human reason is dependent on inductive reasoning then "…almost all our knowledge is only probable."

Laplace imagines a being who knows everything, all the forces of nature and therefore the cause and effect of all actions: "For such an intellect nothing would be uncertain and the future just like the past would be present before its eyes." Laplace's demon is god-like without the beneficence or humanity we tend to ascribe to God; he is also, as I read Laplace, what the human intellect should and can aspire to. Any freshman psychology or philosophy student can rebut Laplace's philosophy, but I am drawn to his elegance and ambition. Laplace believes that science and math—not religion—will one day lead us away from superstition and ignorance and ameliorate the terror that comes from not knowing what will happen next.

But science has not yet delivered on that promise and we still live with the fear of the imagined probable. Perhaps that explains why my father's love of mathematics—and for making predictions—took an odd turn in the 90s and 00s. He became an astrologer. He'd sit for hours solving equations and charting in elaborate and painstaking detail the positions of planets.

His obsession was in part cultural. Astrology is very important in South Asian culture and many members of my highly educated and accomplished family don't act without first consulting an astrologer. The actual system of charting a horoscope is complicated, involving math and calculation and the exact position of planets in relation to each other and the earth, an elaborate system of causation. It's complicated enough to *appear* a science (and, in fact, in the Greek and Ancient Islamic world, astrologers were also astronomers and mathematicians). I think that's why astrology appealed to my father. If medicine was the science that kept pushing him to the West, astrology was the 'science' that kept him rooted in his culture. I remember the charts he drew, a series of concentric and interconnecting circles, that resembled, to my untrained eye, spirographs.

It's easy to scorn my father's obsession, but instead, I try to imagine the level of uncertainty he grappled with, from his life as an immigrant to his career as a doctor.

He contended every day with death, often the deaths of people he'd grown to like and care about. I really can't begrudge him his desire to find some way to forestall and to explain the terrible grief he felt at being displaced, to ease the anxiety of wondering if he had made a mistake-- in a diagnosis, in a cultural slip to a colleague or his own daughter, in leaving his homeland. My father studied astrology for decades and even became certified by the American Federation of Astrology. Last summer, when I was packing up his office, I found the certificate provided by the AFA framed and hanging on the wall across from all his diplomas and medical certifications placed so that he would be able to see it every day from his desk as he worked.

Survivors

LIEUTENANT MATTOCKS BECAME the first person to survive a jump from an overhead hatch of an airplane. Major Tulloch, to the disbelief of those on the ground, came stumbling out of a Goldsboro swamp covered in mud, unharmed. Five members of the crew lived; three died. Even if you've never heard about the Goldsboro "broken arrow," you know the end of this story. The two hydrogen bombs did not detonate, though according to military records one bomb came close. Five of the six arming devices had been activated.

One of the bombs was recovered intact. The second fell into a swamp. The bomb sank deeper into the mud and the military was only able to make a partial retrieval. The rest remains buried in the ground in Faro a few miles from Goldsboro.

The U.S. military created different designations for a variety of potential nuclear incidents. "Broken arrow" is the term for an accidental or near detonation. There have been thirty-two broken arrows globally and three in the United States. My sister sent me a link to the original *Guardian* article, published in 2013, detailing journalist Eric Schlosser's work to uncover more about what happened in Goldsboro. Her accompanying message was one line: *How different our lives would be if the bomb went off and we went back to SL instead of going to Goldsboro.* Though I recognize it's the human condition to wonder what might have been, it's the immigrant's particular condition to live always with the idea that you might have lived a parallel life, been someone else completely.

I'm awed by the risks our government took, the short-sightedness, the willingness to place us in jeopardy. For all the talk of Russia's threat, we were just as likely—perhaps more likely—to have blown *ourselves* up. Still, any good writing workshop stresses that a tragedy averted does not make for a particularly impactful story. We want weighted consequences to our actions, and if we manage to find our footing in the swamp and stumble out intact, we should pat ourselves on the back and move on.

But what about the verity of those stories we tell ourselves? The stories that buttress our fears and justify the risks we take? I remember *The Day After* and *Red Dawn*. I sang along to the radio, "I hope the Russians love their children too." I remember going to bed believing the Russians would bomb us as I slept. I never knew an American nuclear warhead was buried just miles from my bedroom. No, I wouldn't have slept any better, but I would have known something closer to the truth.

A great many people are constantly taking risks with their lives, with our lives, with my life. Each of us takes our own risks in near darkness. We all might as well be Laplace's primitive man staring at the sky in awe, believing that the comet is an omen.

The Demon

MY FATHER ASSIDUOUSLY monitored his health his whole life. Diabetes runs in his family and his father, my grandfather, passed away in his fifties from a heart attack. He ran. He built a weight room in his basement. He watched his diet. Yet, when his physician suggested he take a blood thinner for his atrial fibrillation he decided against it. He was very healthy, active, and very low risk. He also, given his family history, was more afraid of a heart attack. He believed he would be able to sense an arrhythmia.

He suffered a massive stroke a year ago that left his body partially paralyzed and his brain shattered. He can no longer read. He's easily confused and he requires twenty-four hour care. He finds it difficult to speak in English even though before the stroke he was bilingual. I overheard his caretaker the other day carefully explaining the days of the week to him. He regularly mentions a visitor who as far as we can tell doesn't exist. He wants a dog with a childlike fervor, but we can't buy him one because he cannot care for himself much less an animal.

I learned of my father's decision not to take the medicine while he was in the hospital after the stroke. It angers me that my father counted on luck in such a way. I also realize when I second-guess my father's decision, I am pretending at being Laplace's demon. I think about those men at SAC guessing and second-guessing their decisions and recognize I'm engaging in my own strange and clumsy pas de deux with life's events. We can't ever *know*. Arthur Schopenhauer in *World as Will and Presentation* quotes ancient Vedic philosophy when trying to define the mind's relationship to its present: "'It is Maya the veil of deception that envelopes the eyes of mortals, lets them see a world of which one can say neither that it is nor that it is not; for it is like a dream, like the reflection of the sun on the sand that the wanderer takes from afar as for water, or a rope thrown down that one sees as a snake.'"

I don't recognize this man my father has become. I'm guessing he could live like this for a long time, or not, and I'm scared of the future either way. My father doesn't speak much anymore to my sisters or to me because we can't converse in Sinhala. He speaks a great deal to his caretaker. One day, my sister wanted to know what they were talking about. I admitted to eavesdropping. My Sinhala isn't very good but I think she was telling him stories. The narratives sounded like bedtime stories, and he didn't respond, only listened. After a moment, feeling the intruder, realizing I didn't really understand anyway, I turned and tiptoed away.

Works consulted:

Dobson, Joel. *The Goldsboro broken arrow: the B-52 crash of January 24, 1961, Goldsboro, North Carolina: the story of the men on the sharp end.* Greensboro, NC: J. Dobson, 2011.

Laplace, Pierre-Simon De, and Andrew I. Dale. *Philosophical essays on probabilities.* New York: Springer, 1995.

Myers, Caron. "The Night Hydrogen Bombs Fell on North Carolina." *Our State.* 29 May 2012. Web.

Schopenhauer, Arthur, David Carus, and Richard E. Aquila. *Arthur Schopenhauer: the world as will and presentation.* Upper Saddle River, NJ: Prentice Hall, 2011.

DILRUBA AHMED

Given Substance

ORIGIN mid 17th cent.: from medieval Latin
substantiat- 'given substance,' *from the verb* substantiare.

I. Independent Commission Report, Version 1

"The Wide-Ranging Deleterious Consequences of Substance X"

After six years of independent research, our findings
have linked Substance X to a variety of undesirable
effects. The least of which is not the soil and water
contamination. Endocrine disrupters, carcinogens.
Make note of birth defects, unexpected heart failure,
climate change, premature deaths. Alternative
industry approaches are available with lower cost
to our environment, our wallets, and our health.
In short, this committee's assessment supports
swift and drastic action. Given the considerable
risks, we must ban all use of Substance X.

II. Independent Commission Report, Version 2

"Cleaner Technology Substitutes Assessment for Professional,
Industrial, and Medical Processes"

After consulting with our partners at the Center
for Risk Analysis, the Coalition for Sustainable
Development, the Council on Competitiveness,
the Chamber of Formaldehyde, the Chemical Industry
Institute of Toxicology, and the Association
of Synthetic Organic Chemical Manufacturers, our
committee has concluded that, while some safety risks
may be linked with continued use of Substance X,

our findings do not warrant immediate action.
For the sake of public health, our committee
must disclose that, very rarely, some consumers
may experience mild irritation upon contact
with Substance X. Other effects include
unstoppable hair growth. Ingrown
toenails. Increased body odor. So rare
are such cases, they are rendered insignificant
(which validates this half-page text, conveyed
without fanfare, outside the pressure
of the press). As such, our findings support
continued use. Given the lack of substantiated
safety risks, we cannot justify changes
in policy. In fact, our findings suggest the benefits
of Substance X may have been under-realized,
as they are many, and they are diverse. Of course,
all findings will be subject to future commission
assessment. For now, when considering standard
practice, we have neither objections nor concerns.

JOHN GALLAHER

It's Not About What We Want, But About Figuring Out What's Worth Wanting

The other day my dog, our dog, the family dog, looked back at me
from the landing on the stairs. It's as far up as he's allowed to go.
And he looked blankly at me and I looked blankly back at him.
And then he winked. I winked back. I like to think we just had a
moment. "Yep, I'm as far as I can go." "Yep, you are." You have
to believe to stay where you are and you have to believe to get places.
"Something will happen," we say to each other. It will be good. But
journeys ebb. What was fine imagining with the promises of genie
wishes becomes three more things from your list of demented things.
Honor paints the walls a faint green. Maybe it's gray. Because the total
mass/energy of the universe is zero, as I read the other day, it makes
perfect sense that the overheard misery date that's coming apart outside
my office should be taking place over the phone. "Well, I've never
homewrecked anyone," X is saying to Y, in the hall. "It'll do you good,"
we say to each other at various times. Like these, for instance. But
according to whose plan? Like what, how running does you good?
And what if running kills you? Michael was running in a half marathon
yesterday in St. Joseph, and his leg broke. Stress fracture. It just came
apart beneath him. What if some of these good ideas are terrible ideas?
History is not kind to our good ideas. The leeches leech too much. The
prayer just keeps us from getting to the hospital in time. The vitamin C
poisons you. There was a guy who only ate carrots, a monofoodie, and
he turned orange and wondered why he was dying. We must go out for
fresh air until outside air is industrial, and then it's "stay indoors and get
a purifier and a generator" if you're living in Baoding in Hebei province,
in China, 140 kilometers to the northeast of Beijing. Maybe that's what
we're thinking over the primordial soup we decided to try for something
different. Maybe it'll do us good, as we'll probably never be able to make
detailed predictions of complex systems, we can at least, what, go to a
restaurant, I guess. Or try a new move out to impress ourselves on our
first date. I used coupons on a first date once, as it's a wide array, even

at Pizza Hut. So we get a pet. Have kids. And time's arrow gets us to a hallway, and here's a donut. The first placental mammal is currently hypothetical, and climbed trees, eating insects, weighing between six and 245 grams. It gave birth to one hairless baby at a time. After that, we call it "fumbling." And one would think to add "in the dark," but that would be wrong. It's bright here. Options are everywhere. Brilliance.

JOSEPH O. LEGASPI

Hamburger

*"The great curse of American food culture
is that we have no food culture."*
—Chef Dan Barber

In 1984, when I arrived in these United States, pastel neon,
in the dream pastiche desert of Olympics-fisted Los Angeles,
I wanted my first meal to be a hamburger, drenched in tomato—
not banana—ketchup, squeezed between white sesame seed
buns, not *pan de sal*, Filipino morning roll eaten sweetly
any time of the day. That had to wait. On arrival in a town
called Bell I was served rice under pork-chicken adobo,
and the rest of my first week a feast as if I'd never left:
pancit garnished with shredded veggies for longevity;
oxtails, pork hocks, calves feet bisque in peanut butter
sauce; pig stewed in shrimp paste; bitter melon, chayote,
achiote. The women lived practically in the kitchen, how
things had not yet changed, my grandmother chopping,
stir-frying, frying, boiling, steaming, mashing, melodious
sounds that carry the bewildering loneliness of a foreign
home momentarily out of doors. Since the table was not
big enough, we ate together scattered throughout the
two-bedroom-one-bath house shared by three families.
On mats on the floor, we children loved sleeping side-
by-side, hotdogs rotating on a carnival seller's grill. But I
was growing impatient, the fast food that would transform
me into an American I hadn't ingested, a kind of superhero
pill. Until my first day of school in my 7th grade cafeteria
where I was served a round patty of compressed meat,
boiled, charred, yawning open-faced next to curly potatoes
glowing a cartoon meteorite orange. I could not contain
my joy, I tore and poured on packets of ketchup, discarded
the wilted iceberg like fabric softener, clamped the hamburger

between my shaky hands and chomped momentously into my first taste of America. Salty, starchy, chewy beginning to a lifetime consumption, powdered with sugar, melted as margarine, deep fried, blue-dyed, iced over, Jell-oed, marshmallowed, popcorned, bite-sized, on-the-run.

Culture

Not to make yogurt with.

Albeit it can be derived from ancient strain
passed down through generations of men
and women alchemizing milk.

Culture is to make do and plenty of a place.
Rituals from routines, meaning
erupting from nothing.

Eating holy swine from knuckles to ear-tips.
Praying to the pickling gods of fermentation.
Digging deep for tubers, roots that bind
the whole of the land.

Blood and sky and feet and flight and pride.

Children speak of it, and sing.
It fills their stomachs as they travel.

LESLEY WHEELER

Cave Painter, Dordogne

After sketching ten thousand churning forelegs
in river sand—after hunt, slaughter, dinner
taught lessons in muscle and bone—your hand
has earned the curve of a bison's back.

Fat is smeared in concave rocks to burn
with juniper wicks; you've powdered ochre,
chewed a bit of hide soft for a sponge.
No longer young. Every joint groans

while you climb the scaffolding. Then,
as pupils slowly widen, you forget
the smoking griefs and pursue shadow.
Whole herds await release. That stalactite,

a tail. Rocky dimple, a horse's belly:
starved to the touch, but to the eye, as replete
with secrets as a mare in foal. Next
blow a mist of pigment through hollow bone

and each sooty line is true the first time.
That third-best aurochs might survive
seventeen thousand years while its livelier kin
wash down a wall, silting like ghosts into

la Vézère, but on a good day you don't care.
Finding can be happier than keeping.
What I can't fathom is where you hope
they're going, the queues of rusty bulls

and horses. Or is it the same horse, over
and over, in motion? It leaps into the dark,
or crawls. Each beast with work
to unearth, deep in the limestone.

ANDREW CARTWRIGHT

Aglossiac

There was a man who had no tongue, or his tongue was too small, no tongue to speak of, or he'd had a tongue before he cut it out one day for feeling too much, lumbering glumly behind his teeth, always worrying his gums to weeping, or he'd cut it down to the stump for feeling like too much, weighing him down like a pregnant belly, swelling up like a puffer fish, or he was born with no tongue, born empty and unsound, or his tongue simply got lost amidst the quick streams surrounding him, a broken oar lapping aimlessly, or his tongue grew tired of him, felt too tied down, uprooted itself to search for better stories, or it doesn't matter, his tongue was just dead, he didn't want to talk about it, or he swallowed his tongue just to see if he could, or his tongue was bitten off by a lusty cannibal ex, or his tongue was made of gold and he didn't want to share, or his tongue was an uninflated air balloon and he was too afraid of heights to open his mouth, or his tongue was theoretically nothing but a word, conceptualized but never realized, or he somehow discovered that his tongue had only one utterance left and he wanted to choose a good one, but the only thing that ever came to mind was "bitter," or he's such a good listener, or he's just real shy, or he's a man, what're you going to do, or he does seem distant, or is he hiding something, or he's so angry all the time, or if he hates me, he should just say it, or you hate me, just say it, just say it, I hate you too, or you don't love me anymore, you don't, I know it's true, you don't even have to say it.

ELIZABETH SCANLON

Still Life

The chair longs for the table
but someone is always coming between them.
They don't even touch. Or barely, sometimes,
a shoulder-to-shoulder lean, a backwards bump.
The table wears its age better, no surprise, having been
sat upon less, though it carries weight. The chair
creaks all the time. Is coming apart at the joints.
Longs for the old night club days when,
after closing, they'd stack ass to face
and rest that way till the next day.

ADRIAN C. LOUIS

The Hermit's Diary

1. Age has withered my rage. The roiling, molten core of my youth has cooled into dull, cold metal. Nevertheless, sometimes I grab a butter knife & dance around the kitchen, threatening the sluggish Mr. Coffee machine.

2. I grew up in a shack. I lived in an 8x10 closet off the front porch of an old railway house. Me, my cot, some small shelves on one wall where my mom stacked my clean clothes. I hid out there most days to avoid the cruel, white demon that was my stepfather. I waited in the oppressive air of desert afternoons for him to leave for the swing shift at the copper mine.

 Decades later, I rise in another shack of a house at five in the morning, make coffee, putter around until the early afternoon heat creeps up on me. Then I turn on the air conditioning & go to bed. When I am shivering from the cold, I pull the blankets up & take a nap. I have worked my whole life for such peace.

3. Escaping the glare of the computer, I find myself motoring past my former place of employment. I soak up the summertime college mist like an old, dry sponge. Tan girls taking remedial courses are lounging upon the lawns. Firm bottoms & bellies & heads filled with helium. America. The smell of sun tan lotion simmering on young women's skin. Driving past the hospital, I inhale the hot tar a road crew is laying down. I love the smell of tar. One desert summer, I worked as a flagman for a paving company. Then, I had a firm bottom & belly. My head was not filled with helium but small, happy clouds of incinerated flora.

TALIA BLOCH

You Will Go Out

The companion of the morning is silence:
a caged, iron silence that brings on a seasickness
on dry land.
            The night had guests who stayed late,
then left. The night had strange guests who laughed
over my wine and eggs, flashing their large teeth.

Now, in the morning, I stand at the mirror
examining my face for lines, combing my wet hair,
shaking out the drops.
                I go into the kitchen
and see my neighbor from the window
standing on the sidewalk. His is an industrious life.
He takes a chair from his truck and brings it
into the house. He brings his children out for school,
their sandwiches tucked in bags under his arm.

Last night it was warm. Today it is already fall.
The trees look bloodied by the change, girded
to conquer, yet already succumbing.

Last night I lay on top of the blanket after the guests
had gone and felt a breeze float through the room.
Belly soft. Fingers warm.
                Now I steady myself against a wall,
pull on my boots, pull tight my coat. A thousand feet
are running to the trains, a thousand motors are rushing by,
transporting hearts and hands through the streets
in metal bins. I will myself. I say it's fine. This is the way it is.
Must always have been. I say, you will. You will go out.

Translation Folio

PAYAM YAZDANJOO

Translator's Introduction

Poupeh Missaghi

"Mantra" is part of Bombay *Rain,* a collection of interrelated short stories, all set in India, where Payam Yazdajoo lived for five years as a graduate student.

I was asked by Payam if I would translate the stories while he was still working on the final edits of the book. He had not yet submitted them to Iranian publishers and had some hesitations about whether to do it or not. He was, however, eager to try the chances of the stories individually and the collection in translation aiming for publication with English-language outlets either in India or elsewhere.

I read the whole collection and if I remember correctly we decided to start with translating three stories, including "Mantra."

An interesting aspect of the stories that made me eager to work on them was that the project had an inherently multi-translational nature. Here was Payam, an Iranian author and translator living in India as a graduate student, working alongside me, another Iranian author and translator living in the US to translate a collection of short stories set in India, written in Persian, to be translated into English. Also, the stories themselves dealt with the issue of translation from various angles, weaving together linguistic, cultural, and historical aspects of the two countries and beyond.

"Bombay Rain," the first story I translated from the collection, which was published in *The Denver Quarterly* (Vol. 48, No. 3, 2014), is the story of a group of friends attempting to make a film inspired by *The Blind Owl,* the most famous novel of Iranian author Sadegh Hedayat, who committed suicide in Paris in 1951.

"Mantra," the story you are going to read, is about two Iranian friends in India setting themselves up to translate the *Gita Govinda,* an Indian text from nine hundred years ago. In order to do so, they need a mediator language, since none can read Sanskrit. So they decide to "get help from a selection of reliable English translations, compare the translations, and reach our own conception of the text." Concepts of text, originality, commentary, interpretation, and translation are some of the main themes of the story. Linguistic transference weaves together with identity fluidity, temporal and geographical uncertainty, death and reincarnation.

All stories of the collection, moreover, combine reality with illusion, the natural with the supernatural, moving back and forth between one world and another, as does translation.

Another interesting aspect of the project came to be the fact that the originals were not yet published but in the final phase of editing, in other words not, yet completely done. Working on each story, I realized there were concerns I needed to raise with Payam. These were not merely linguistic or cultural concerns or questions, but instances that did not sound right or make sense in the story world. There were also places where everything in the original worked but then discussions to find the perfect English choice brought attention to subtleties in the original that could still be further tweaked. We spent hours on Skype, discussing a verb choice, a tense, a subject in a long sentence, a sequence of events, cadences, rhythms, etc.

In a way, my translating process, demanding a close reading and excavating of the text in the original Persian, came to add another layer to Payam's editing process, taking it deeper and deeper. Moreover, his edited Persian drafts along with his close readings and evaluations of the English translation once again demanded me to go further with scrutinizing, editing, and aiming to perfect the English.

Throughout the back and forth process of translating "Mantra," it was as if the stories were trying to continuously write and rewrite themselves in the two languages, the original Persian and the secondary English, simultaneously. It was as if they wanted to remind us that there is no one definite final text, which, as you will see in the story, perfectly suites the nature of "Mantra" and its world, as it does the whole concept and nature of *translation*.

Mantra

MANI HAD INVITED ME TO go to Delhi. I had not seen him since my arrival in India one year ago. During the time, we kept in touch by long letters and from time to time by very short phone conversations. We had finished translating the *Gita* and the principal *Upanishads* two years before, and our ideas for a next collaboration had not gotten anywhere. I had suggested working on the *Puranas;* and Mani, the *Gita Govinda*. We set out to read the works but, finding none of them attractive enough, had not come to any conclusions. Now Mani suggested we spend the month together to work. He had just finished his masters and was soon to return to Iran, and I was moving to Bombay in a month or two. The airport was less crowded than I had expected. I waited an hour for Mani so that we could go to his humble flat near Connaught Place. We spent the night catching up and the next day we got busy reviewing the texts.

We tackled the *Puranas* for a week and did not get anywhere. Eighteen volumes with vast commentaries were too voluminous to be translated into Persian. Translating the more famous volumes such as the *Vishnu Purana* or the *Bhagavata Purana* did not make sense. The *Gita Govinda* seemed a better choice. It was not as ancient as the *Puranas*, it had been written some nine hundred years ago, but had the advantage of being shorter, had a well-known author, Jayadeva, and content-wise was more coherent and even, in some aspects, more interesting to us. We started with the original versions but realized early on that our Sanskrit was not good enough for the task. Neither Mani nor I knew enough Sanskrit to be able to read and understand the *Gita Govinda* without a mediator. We thought it best to follow the method we had previously used for the *Gita* and the *Upanishads*: to get help from a selection of reliable English translations, compare the translations, and reach our own conception of the text.

We listed the existing English translations: from the first by Sir William Jones in 1792 to the last by Barbara Stoler Miller in 1977. We spent a few days looking for them and we found a few. We read them side by side, but this too was to no avail. The translators' interpretations were so different from one another that we could not find any clear correspondence between them and the original Sanskrit. We had almost renounced the whole project when we suddenly came upon a more recent translation by Narayana, published five years ago. It was so fluent that it engraved the main story and all the details in our minds in a single reading. Following a lengthy introduction,

Narayana had dissected every verse with incredible patience. First came the original text in Sanskrit in Devanagari script, then the text again in Sanskrit but this time in Latin script, then the English translation, and finally an analysis of the text. This had, however, doubled or tripled the length of the Sanskrit verse, and that was problematic for us. We were not looking for an interpretive translation. We needed a literal translation to get us closer to the Sanskrit original. It seemed that the solution was with none but with Narayana himself.

Shri Shrimad Bhaktivedanta Narayana Maharaja was born in a Brahmin family in a village in Bihar in 1921. In his childhood, he constantly murmured the names of the Gods and had the *Mahabharata* and the *Ramayana* and other sacred stories memorized. As a young man, he met with Shrila Narottamananda Brahmachari, one of the missionaries of the Gaudia Vedanta Samiti. Narayana spent day and night listening to Narottamananda and his attendants reciting stories of the Gods to the people of Bihar. Following his correspondence with Shrila Bhakti Prajnana Kesava Maharaja, known as Gurudeva or Guru Maharaja, he left his home and family and joined the Vishnavite storytellers. Gurudeva, taking him along on his journey around India, shared with him one of Vishnu's names and taught him the mantra that let him be received by the Gods. He then offered Narayana the sanyasi monk robe, letting him personally choose the rod to go with the robe. Between the Mayavadi straight rod and the Bhakti trident, Narayana chose the latter and thus strengthened his bond with Gurudeva. And Gurudeva chose the wandering hermit storyteller as the headmaster of the Shri Kesavaji Gaudia School in Mathura. A few years later, Narayana met, in Calcutta, with Shrila Bhaktivedanta Swami Prabhupada, founder of the International Society for Krishna Consciousness, who years later came to stay in Mathura for some six months. Swami then moved to the United States and opened the first Radha-Krishna temple there, and later Narayana had to take charge of Swami's funeral in Vrindavan. Later on, Narayana also left for several countries, spreading the Krishna religion, and he had his works translated into dozens of languages. Eventually he returned to Mathura, settled in a grand and glorious temple, and resumed publishing his analyses and translations of Vishnu-Krishna works.

We knew where we needed to go. We had to get to Mathura before it was too late.

"We might not find anything, but we won't lose anything either. I don't mind seeing Vrindavan and Gowardhan one more time. And you can get busy taking photographs," Mani said.

This was my first trip in India since my return. It was to be Mani's last. From Delhi to Mathura, it was not more than three or four hours. We rented a car and set off. Much of the road was under construction, dug up here and there. We reached

Mathura at dusk. We found a hotel and, rather than going out to wander around, we decided to stay in and prepare for the next day.

The next morning we left the hotel with no clear minds, simply heading for the Yamuna River. The water was high, making it impossible to get to the other side. Mud was everywhere and we could not even walk to the staircases that had gone under water. We decided to head to the bazaar and the small temples on our side of the river, hoping to find another way to get to the great temple. We had only taken a few steps when a boatman stopped us, offering us a free ride on the river. It seemed a common trick for snaring tourists, but we did not say no. The boatman also picked up an old woman and an old man and the five of us sat in the rowboat. The river was too muddy to reveal its depth, but the ride did not seem too risky. The old man got off a hundred steps farther, went up to his waist in the water, moved towards the muddy riverbank, and was lost behind the mud cottages. When we reached a temple drowned in the middle of the river, the old woman got up, opened a box, spread ashes of a deceased in the water, and sat down again. The boatman followed the coastline and the old woman got off at the foot of a staircase. He took money neither from the old man nor from the old woman.

With only the two of us left in the boat, we offered the boatman money to take us to the other side. He did not budge but allowed that we could stay on the river as long as we wanted, and he would take us back when we were done. In the Indian style, he had no rush to do anything, even to make money. Dozens of meters farther, next to an almost dry staircase, he stopped to pee. Mani was reading a book on the Vishnu Bhakti rituals. I had brought out my camera and was taking photos.

"Did you know that according to Vishnu's followers Krishna is not Vishnu's re-incarnation?" Mani asked.

"How come?"

"They believe Vishnu is Krishna's reincarnation, just like Rama."

I changed the camera lens. "What do the Bhakti people say?"

"They say the same thing, except that they put as much significance on Radha."

I took a photo of Mani and replied with my own piece of wisdom, "Now, listen to this wisdom! Did you know that you and I have forever been reading Maha Mantra wrongly?"

"How come?" Mani asked, laughing.

"I realized this just last night. I read it in one of Narayana's books, when you were asleep. You and I always say Hari Krishna. The right way to say it is Hare Krishna."

"Good, but what's the wisdom in that?"

"Hare means both Hari, the name of Vishnu / Krishna, and Hara, which is the name of Radha."

Mani burst out laughing again and snapped, "Got it! Wrote it!"

I joined him in his laughter. "It's already written! I myself will take its virginity!" I said.

The boatman returned to the boat and pointed to what was going on behind us. Six boys sat on top of a temple, their legs dangling in the water. Staring at us, they laughed. We waved to them. The boatman pointed at my camera and signaled to me to take a photo. I took a few shots of them sitting together. Then one of the boys dived into the river. I took another photo. Another kid followed him in. Mani stood next to me, saying *aur, aur,* meaning "next," and with every *aur* another kid dived in the river. I took photos one after another. It seemed there would be no end to it. As soon as the boys reached the water, they went back up from the other side and dived in again, with or without Mani's *aur.* They finally stopped after some ten minutes, and rushed towards the boat. The boatman sent them away with his oar. Mani and I got off at a landing to show the kids their photos. When we were done, the boatman pointed to himself. I took a photo of him too and showed it to him. He laughed and pointed to the other side of the river.

"Are you going to take us to the other side?" I asked.

He did not respond. I took his silence for his sluggishness. Or he could simply be dumb. It did not make much difference. Then, slowly, with no words, he started towards the other riverbank.

When we reached the middle of the river, the boatman stopped rowing and pointed to the temple. As if a thick tree had grown in an instant in the heart of a grove, the temple had risen to the sky. We stared for a few moments and suddenly the temple was not there anymore. It had begun to revolve as if a wandering island around the grove. For a second we thought the boat was caught in a whirlpool, but it was actually standing still and the temple was circling on a fixed orbit, around an unknown center and around itself. The boatman sat on the prow of the boat, took a beedi from his shirt pocket and lighted it. He offered it. Mani did not refuse his hand because he considered any kind of hand-wrapped cigarettes better than all other kinds. I did not smoke beedi. I was sensitive to its dry smoke, so much so that I could not make myself smoke them even when I was poor.

One hour passed. I took photos of our surroundings, Mani read his book, and the boatman remained idle. Done with taking photos, I sat on the floor of the boat and rolled a cigarette for myself. Mani had put the book on his face and fallen silently asleep. The sun shone but was not burning. I too lay down and closed my eyes. First I saw the sun, full and round, in the middle of the black sky, and then the wandering temple.

When I woke the boatman was sitting where he had been all along. Mani was standing, staring at the horizon.

"Get up! Watch eternity, my friend!"

I got up and stood next to him. Fog was spreading over the horizon, and the drowning sun was setting the clouds overhead on fire. The river, crimson and white and blue and purple, was resting in its majestic glory. The sunset seemed an eternal metaphor.

"One day we will return to this eternity with our beloveds," said Mani.

We returned to the hotel in the early hours of the evening. We asked the hotel manager about the temple and heard the expected answer. There was no way to get to the other side of the river for now. When he asked why we were interested in the temple, I explained that we were looking for an author, Narayana, Shri Shrimad Bhaktivedanta Narayana Maharaja. The name rang a bell, but he could not remember anything specific about the person bearing it. We spent the next morning going to some small temples and to the modern temple of Krishna Janmabhoomi, the birthplace of Lord Krishna. There was no sign of Narayana anywhere. The location of Gaudia Vedanta Publishing House also remained unknown to us. It seemed that their office was in Mathura, but no exact address was provided.

The day after, we went wandering in the bazaar and the alleys leading to the Yamuna. Kids played on the railways no longer in service. I took pictures. The large amounts of garbage left there could not go hidden even under the monsoon rain. The stations were homes to heaps of garbage and the tracks had practically become garbage tracks, passing each and every alley, each and every house. There were stations every ten steps. Mani was busy talking with the residents and asking them questions. They all knew hundreds of sadhus and sanyasis and swamis and rishis and maharajas, but none knew Shri Shrimad Bhaktivedanta Narayana Maharaja.

At dusk we went to the Yamuna. The sunset did not have the same charm as the day when we had first watched it over the river, but it still seemed magical. The water had receded, and the mud was fast drying. We spent two or three hours by the river before walking back to the hotel by way of the riverbank. We were in no rush. There was no sign of prayer, music, or singing along the river. There were no candles on the water, no evening bathing in it. As we got to the main street, we noticed the boatman waiting for us.

"Perhaps he regrets yesterday's generosity and is here to take the money he refused," Mani predicted. He brought out some bills and held them towards the boatman. The boatman pushed the money aside with one hand and pointed to the river with the other.

We thought at first that he was offering to take us across. We looked. The other side was emerged in total darkness. The boatman pointed once again, showing us a ruined temple. Next to the temple there was a round platform with several columns topped by multiple crowns. We saw the flickering light of a candle coming from that direction. The shadow of a man fell over the platform.

"Let's try him," Mani suggested.

The man whose shadow we had seen was praying. Facing the Yamuna, he murmured under his breath. We waited until he finished. He was an old man with a long beard and long hair, wearing an orange robe and an orange turban.

He did not look like a boatman, but Mani asked him anyway, "Can you take us to the other side?"

"Of course, I can. Why do you want to get to the other side?" answered the old man in English. Mani had asked in Hindi.

"We want to see the temple," I answered in English.

"Why do you want to see the temple?" asked the man in Hindi.

"We want to meet a Sanyasi," I answered in English.

"Narayana," Mani and I said at the same time. There was no difference in its Hindi and English.

The old man looked us over. He took his trident in hand and stood up.

"You want to meet Narayana?" he asked in Hindi, then continued in English, "Why do you want to meet Narayana?"

"We want to consult him about something," Mani said.

"About a book," I said.

The old man paused, gathered his stuff from the ground, and said, "Narayana is not there."

"Where is he then?" Mani asked.

"Right here! May I help you?" asked Narayana.

We had no reason not to believe him. Mani explained our situation, and we made plans to meet the day after at dusk with a copy of the *Gita Govinda*. He did not seem to fully grasp our concerns, but promised to bring his own copy and help us out. We spent the next morning in Gowardhan, only half an hour from Mathura. We visited some temples and ashrams and returned to Mathura and the Yamuna early in the evening. When we got to the Yamuna the sun was almost set, but there was no sign of Narayana. We came upon the boatman on a platform and asked him about Narayana. He nodded and looked away at another spot. Narayana was sitting there, on another platform farther away. The platform looked similar to the one we were at, but there was a distance of a hundred meters between them. Narayana stood up and waved to us. We waved back.

Sitting cross-legged at a low small desk, Narayana was busy reading and writing comments and marginal notes. We sat nearby and waited for him to finish. He had added so many pages to the original book that it was falling apart. The old man glanced at Mani.

Showing him our copy, Mani announced, "This is the copy we have of your *Gita Govinda*."

"Well, I have got my own copy here," Narayana said and drew a hand over one of the pages of the open book. "Where in the book is your problem?" he asked.

"We have a problem with the whole book," I said.

Narayana threw me a look and went back to reading and taking notes.

"My friend meant to say that our problem is a general one," Mani clarified.

"Can he explain in a clearer way?" he asked without looking up.

"We want to translate your book into our own language," I replied.

Amused or amazed, Narayana looked up at us. "We are colleagues then?"

"Somehow," Mani said.

"So tell me, what is your problem with the whole book?" Narayana asked.

"We are not fluent enough in Sanskrit. To translate into Persian, we depend mostly on your English translation," Mani said.

"You have turned each Sanskrit verse into several English ones. It helps the reader understand the text, but it would be more useful for us to first know the exact equivalents of the Sanskrit words and phrases," I said.

"We need a translation that's not an interpretation," said Mani.

Narayana gave us a confused look. "All translations are interpretations."

"You are a prominent translator and interpreter. But we were just wondering whether you also have a more concise version of the text," I said.

"What do you think I am doing now?" asked Narayana. We did not have an answer. "I am interpreting," he paused, "I am translating that very translation you call interpretive." He handed a section of the beginning of the book to Mani. Mani leafed through it and passed it to me. I too browsed it. Narayana had further expanded his own translation of the first chapter of the *Gita Govinda*. The translation of the four-line verse now added up to fourteen pages, and this was aside from the forty-page interpretation that followed.

"This is wonderful. But we will be thankful if we could also take a look at the older versions of your book," Mani said. "Perhaps they are more concise, in a way, more literal."

"Leave now. Come back tomorrow. I will look through my library. I might find something useful to you," concluded Narayana.

The next day we did not leave the hotel until the afternoon, when it was time for our meeting with Narayana. He was sitting on another platform and was busy working. He took ten minutes to stop.

"Years ago there was a Brahmin who converted to Buddhism, becoming a Bodhisattva, a future Buddha. The Bodhisattva wished to collect all of the Buddha's sayings and write a book entitled *Thus Spoke Buddha*. What do you think his first problem, his main problem was? Throughout time so many dubious words had been attributed to the Buddha that it was primarily necessary to recognize what the Buddha had not said. The Brahmin, the Bodhisattva, spent a lifetime to do just that and never got to writing the book entitled *Thus Spoke Buddha*. What he wrote instead was *Thus Spoke Not Buddha*," said Narayana.

We waited for him to conclude his story or, as we said between ourselves, to reveal his piece of wisdom, but Narayana did not conclude.

He asked Mani, "Where do you think his problem lay?" and me, "Do you know the difference between the non-dualist doctrine, *advaita*, and the dualist doctrine, *dvaita*? Between Mayavadi and Bhakti?" He did not wait for our responses. "The problem with the Brahmin, or the Bodhisattva, or whoever he was, was that he came from the *advaita* and Mayavadi traditions. He thought of everything as illusions, mayas. He considered himself a monotheist. I consider him a nihilist. His logic was neither this nor that, not both this and that. He had understood the *Upanishads*, but not the *Gita*." Finishing the explanation, Narayana stood up, gathered his stuff, took up his voluminous over-annotated *Gita Govinda*, grasped his trident, and added, "His very problem was in his straight rod."

He did not seem disturbed or angry, but left without saying goodbye. Our attempts to get our hands on the translation seemed futile. After a few steps, Narayana, however, stopped, turned towards us, and said, "Think about what I just said. Come back in three days. I have found the first version of my translation. It is a literal interpretation."

We could now spend a couple of days wandering in leisure. The following morning we packed our things and got to Vrindavan in one hour. There, Radhika welcomed us and took us to her family house. It was a grand mansion, and her family was more welcoming than we expected. We were given a superb room, and Radhika promised to spend a couple of days with us. She was a descendant of the Goswamis of Vrindavan. Her father was a well-known Brahmin and once Octavia Paz's Indian translator. She was Mani's classmate in Delhi and was now in Vrindavan to spend her end-of-term holidays with her family. According to Mani, there had been the possibility of a more intimate relationship between them, but neither of them had acted upon that.

Radhika suggested we not rush to see the sights of Vrindavan. We had already heard the stories in Gowardhan and we could see the sights in one or two days. We had lunch and took a nap until the evening. We then went out for a walk along the Yamuna. Here the riverbank was less muddy, the weather was cooler, and the sky seemed bluer. We walked for a while, and on our way back Radhika took us to temples turned into mosques and to mosques once again turned into temples. She showed us remnants of her ancestors, and a poem by Hafiz inscribed on the façade of a temple in ruins.

The following day we visited Vrindavan temples and listened to the usual stories local guides narrated: from the battle between Krishna and Indra in Gowardhan to *Rasa Lila* and the multiplication of Govinda during the dance of Krishna, *Gopala*, with cowherd girls, *Gopis*. Radhika talked about both the Maha Mantra and the Beatles; about John Lennon who had recalled Hare Krishna in his songs; about George Harrison who had collaborated in an album with the Radha-Krishna Temple, explaining that the Temple had once, at the end of the 1960s, been the site of the International Society for Krishna Consciousness in London; about why the Beatles had visited Rishikesh in February of 1968, staying with Maharishi for meditation, then falling away from Maharishi and leaving India three months later once and for all. The stories went on the following day. We walked on the Yamuna bank, and Mani and Radhika talked about their shared interests. The Beatles in India was Radhika's favorite subject and the Beat Generation in India was Mani's. I did not have much interest in either, so I returned to the alleys and the bazaar to take photos of the kids.

Here too, like Mathura, the stores were narrow, dark, and squeezed together; yet the bazaar seemed less crowded. I wandered by myself, taking photos, now and then buying sundries. At noon, while sitting by a tea cart and drinking chai, I eyed a newspaper shop. It was not much different than a junk shop. The newspapers, out of date or not, secondhand or not, were all piled together and sold at the same price. It was not logical but comprehensible. In India no one read newspapers for the news anyway. Newspapers were, like books, a means to pass time. I lighted a cigarette and as I was leaving the shop, I saw Narayana. His photo was on the first page of the *Hindu*. "Shri Shrimad Bhaktivedanta Narayana Maharaja had died at 3 A.M. on Tuesday in Jagannath Temple in Puri," the headline read. The paper quoted the speaker of the International Society for Krishna Consciousness about the memorial service to be held in Mathura. I checked the dates and hurried back home. Mani and Radhika were not back yet. I found them along the Yamuna.

"Narayana is dead," I told Mani.

"We shall go to Mathura, introduce ourselves at his funeral service, and get the book," Mani suggested.

"The service has already passed. He died three months ago, in Puri," I announced.

Radhika left us to check on her family. Mani and I sat down to go over the events and think about all the possibilities. Narayana had most likely died three months ago in Puri. But then who was the man we had met in Mathura? There were different possibilities. He could be a relative of Narayana, his son or his brother, continuing on with his tradition; or he could be another Narayana who was accidentally of the same name or of the same profession as Narayana; or, perhaps he was a charlatan sadhu or a fraud sanyasi who had introduced himself as Narayana.

"We should go back to Mathura," Mani said.

"You stay, I'll go. If he has the book, I'll get it and come back," I suggested. "If he doesn't, we'll find out what's really going on."

Mani insisted we go together.

"I'll come back as soon as possible," I said and left.

I arrived at our meeting point with Narayana an hour before sunset. He was not there. I walked down the riverbank and searched the platforms one by one. Narayana was not on any. On the last platform I saw another sanyasi. He had a paper in front of him and was staring at an unknown point. He turned around and looked at me. It was the boatman, now wearing an orange robe, holding a trident. I began to realize how much he looked like Narayana. I went over all the possibilities once again. The previous boatman, the present sanyasi, could not have been Narayana. Mani and I had seen the two of them at the same time, and we could not both have made a mistake.

I doubted that the boatman would reveal anything, but I addressed him anyhow. "I'm looking for Narayana."

"I am not Narayana. I am Nara," he said.

My mind was put at ease. "I had thought so. My friend and I were supposed to meet with the man who called himself Narayana."

"You have come for the book?" Nara asked.

I sat down facing him. "So the book is with you?" I said.

"No. But you don't need to worry. Narayana Maharaja's book was not that concise anyway," Nara said.

"Has he told you why we need the book?" I asked.

"The translation was good but not the best. The number of the words in the English translation might have matched those in the original Sanskrit, but that was all."

"What do you think is the best translation?"

"I don't know about the best translation, but I know that my translation is much better than his."

I glanced at the papers in front of him. "Your translation?"

"I am the person who wrote *Thus Spoke Not Buddha*," said Nara.

"So you are a translator too."

"Not the type that you are."

"What's our type?"

"Narayana's. You translate books from older languages into newer ones, from the more dead languages into the more living ones. Your translations are moreover interpretive. Your books naturally always turn out thicker than the originals."

"And what's yours?"

"I translate books into the older languages. Thus my achievements are shorter than yours!"

"Shorter?"

"Yes, shorter! Writing *Thus Spoke Not Buddha* was my internship. I had to write it to arrive at the end, only to get there and realize that there was no end and that I had to once again return to the beginning. It was at that moment that I decided I had to save the heritage of today's and yesterday's generations for the preceding ones."

It was no new thinking. One of the first things any curious person arriving in India learns is that the word for yesterday and tomorrow are one and the same, as is the word referring to the day before yesterday and the day after tomorrow, also the word for the day before the day before yesterday and the day after the day after tomorrow.

"So you too are of the belief that we return to the past?" I asked.

"No, we arrive at the past in the future. Therefore it is much better to have the works of the future at hand when we arrive at the past."

His logic seemed reasonable. "Have you translated the *Gita Govinda* too?" I asked.

"Yes, do you want to hear it?"

"Hear it?"

"Why not? Your type translates the written word to the written word or the oral to the written. I translate the oral to the oral, or the written to the oral."

Nara told me to sit facing Yamuna, in a meditation pose, cross-legged, with my eyes closed. I sat and closed my eyes.

"Concentrate," he said.

A few minutes later he asked me to open my eyes: There was only the Yamuna in front of me. All of a sudden I heard Nara open his mouth and a gentle flood of words floated over my head, lasting only a few seconds. I closed my eyes and opened them again. I did not know the individual meanings of those floating words, I did not know the meaning of them together, but I was certain about one thing: I could feel them with all my being. I had heard the *Gita Govinda*! I had no doubt that what I had heard was the *Gita Govinda*, in its totality, with nothing lost.

"This was the Gita Govinda Mantra." I was still in shock. "Do you want to see the temple on the other side of the river?" Nara asked.

"My friend and I are together and he is not here now," I said.

"I know where he is. Don't worry about him now," said Nara.

I looked at the Yamuna. A heavy rain had started, and the river was unnaturally turbulent. Nara had tied the boat with a long rope to the side of the platform. The boat floated, moving constantly up and down some ten meters from the riverbank.

"From now on my name is Manu, and Manu will guide you through this tempest," said Manu and added, "Take off your shirt!"

I took off my shirt. I knew that to enter grand temples, visitors had to bare their torsos.

Manu took out an orange robe from his sack, "Wear this." I looked at it uncertainly. "This robe is fire. It will burn whatever is inside you and protect you against whatever is outside you."

I wrapped the robe around me. Manu took my hand and led me to the boat.

He sat in the boat and said, "Free the rope."

I untied the rope and got in the boat through the waves and the rain.

A drunken ark in wavy waters, the boat floated forward.

Manu rowed with all his might, shouting "Maha Mantra!" I barely heard him. "Sing Maha Mantra!"

I sang Maha Mantra. *Hare Krishna, Hare Krishna, Krishna Krishna Hare Hare, Hare Rama Hare Rama, Rama Rama Hare Hare.* But the tempest was stronger than to be defeated easily by the mantra. We had reached the middle of the river when the boat was caught in a black whirlpool. Manu stopped rowing. The boat was turning around in a small circle. Out of fear or excitement, I did not tire of singing the Maha Mantra. It seemed to be our only salvation amidst the chaos. *Hare Krishna, Hare Krishna, Krishna, Krishna Krishna Hare Hare.*

"*Om*! *Om*! Only *Om*! Quietly, slowly! *Om*!" Manu advised.

We continued murmuring *Om* until the boat was free of the whirlpool and we were able to continue on our journey. Away from the whirlpool, the Yamuna was unexpectedly quiet. It was still raining, but there were no signs of the tempest anymore.

"Do you think a mantra more concise than *Om* can exist?" Manu asked.

"Isn't *Om* the mother of all mantras?" I asked in response.

Manu stopped rowing for a second. "It exists. It should exist," he said, continuing to row.

"*Om* is just one word," I said.

"A word, but it has one vowel and one consonant," Manu expanded. The rain continued lashing over us. "There is a mantra, there are mantras that are composed of only one vowel!" The fog had begun to descend. I could not see Manu anymore.

"A pure voice," he shouted. "The language of the eternity," he shouted. "The song of the origin," he shouted.

The fog disappeared all of a sudden, the rain stopped, and the water calmed. Manu let go of the oars and, stepping aside to sit down on the prow of the boat, said, "The oars are yours now."

"Who was the sanyasi we saw?" I asked, "What was his relationship to Narayana?"

"He was Narayana," Manu said.

"Narayana died three months ago in Puri," I objected.

Manu did not reply. He was meditating. On the other side of the river, the temple, showered in light and delight, once again rose from the water and soil. As I rowed directly towards it, it started again to turn around itself.

"The man you met was the mantra I have sung. Narayana's Mantra," Manu announced.

"Was he an illusion? Unreal?" I asked.

Manu did not respond. He took the oars, let the boat float towards the bank, and tied it to one of the platforms. I got off the boat.

"From now on my name is Purusha," said Purusha.

The island was empty. There was only the temple glowing in the center in an unbelievable glory.

"You shall not look. You shall not speak a word," said Purusha. I looked at him, not uttering a word. "I am going to follow you but you shall not look back. If you say anything, our companionship will come to an end."

I did not look at him. I did not say a word. I walked towards the temple. Purusha followed, murmuring, and his unclear words, like a flood of broken candles, took me to the temple. There was no one outside the temple, and no sound came from inside. Purusha continued to murmur, following me. He became silent as I arrived at the temple. I stopped, opened the gate, and froze in my place. The fog covered the temple. Nothing could be seen. I heard Purusha's song behind me. Like dancing curtains, the first layers of fog parted before my eyes. I saw Krishna and a large crowd of devotees bowing at his feet. Their prayer, their *puja*, was not accompanied by any music or singing. The only music was Purusha's singing following behind me. The fog cleared further, and I walked forward. I saw Krishna's sixty-four qualities and one hundred and eight gates corresponding to his one hundred and eight names. Purusha was singing another mantra, a mere combination of vowels. I paused and looked up at the sky. No stars, no moon, no clouds. Purusha was silent for a moment and then voiced a single syllable. There was an explosion. The sky became the sky and the moon became the moon and the cloud became the cloud and the star became the star. Now Purusha's voice preceded me and I followed in its footsteps. The voice passed through a cistern, reached a jeweled pavement, and entered a fortress. On the other side of the fortress, I saw a palace of mirrors, with a Maharaja sitting all alone on the veranda. Farther on, I saw a jungle of a thousand crystal trees, with the Buddha naked amongst a group of monks, a meadow crowded with the dying on pyres and on garbage piles, and a hill from which the crucified Christ was descending. Purusha murmured, and I walked farther and farther. Behind the jungle, I saw a city as elegant as Indian music, ponds of Orissa and country lanes of Kerala, tall towers surrounded by clouds of heaving silence, the green coast of Goa and the disgraced saints. I saw the smoke in Benares, the rain in Bombay. I saw myself wandering in a square, asking the passersby their names, the passersby asking me mine. Wandering, I ran on a road of voidness. I was lost and I was seeing my being lost. I could not turn around and look behind me. I could still hear Purusha. I saw Meenakshi going far away. I saw Vrindavan and the six Goswamis of Vrindavan. I saw Radhika coming towards me and I heard Mani's shadow calling out my name.

I too called out to him, "Mani!"

The fog returned and drowned everything in it. I turned around. No voice could be heard. There was no sign of Purusha. The gate of the temple, a hundred meters from me, was wide open. I walked towards it through the fog. I closed it, and in an instance the fog disappeared. I turned around and took a look at the temple.

"Don't worry, those were all my mantras," Purusha shouted. He was standing a few steps from me next to the boat. I reached him, and he asked, "Do you want to know what an illusion is, and what a reality?"

Manu answered him, "One can write an illusion, but not a reality," and did not speak a word more until we arrived at the other side of the river. I got off the boat.

"Don't worry. You'll once again see all that you saw. Next time, alone," said Nara.

Mathura had gone hidden in the fog. The rain fell incessantly. Mani was waiting for me in Vrindavan. I was late.

translated from the Persian by Poupeh Missaghi

JOEL MORRIS

The Guide

THE THREE MEN LODGED IN the hotel, an old brick building built in 1886 with a Mansard-roofed tower facing Main Street. Outside it was still elegant, but the hotel's insides had fallen into disrepair. Yellowing wallpaper, carpets worn into inky footpaths. Too true for Tinseltown, one might say. In fact, the first night of their stay, over vodka martinis at the scuffed mahogany bar, the location manager pointed out a strip of unglued wallpaper and mused that the hotel should be torn down and something more modern built in its place. The director of photography and the screenwriter disagreed. There was something about the decline of a western boomtown tucked between folds of mountains that appealed to both the eye and the imagination.

They were there—the location manager, the director of photography, and the screenwriter—to make a movie. The studio had sent them to scout the place for a western. And it seemed about right. Main Street was out of a studio lot, a line of buildings with their flat false fronts, bright doors and arched windows gaping at one another across a wide bowed street that stretched up from the valley ranchland to the mountains. On small side roads, brightly painted mini-Victorians with gabled porches housed the residents, rustics who offered brief but unrevealing smiles to the visitors.

Despite its beauty it was claustrophobic, this little town. Behind those smiles, behind the storefronts that used to harbor saloons and brothels, the mountains loomed, towered almost a mile above a man's head. Sunlight was brief. Shadows fell by three. Every afternoon clouds curtained the peaks, hemmed in the hamlet like a fairytale where something wicked wended its way down. Through the clouds poked the pinion pines that had somehow staggered themselves along the red cliff walls, where in the mist an itinerant mountain goat might also appear, like a white snowflake, barely visible to the untrained eye.

It was Gunderson who pointed out the goat. Gunderson, himself out of place— his accent was as Midwestern as his name—was their host, the man who'd made the arrangements. He was the nervous sort, obviously ill at ease with "you Hollywood boys," as he kept calling them. In each conversation he managed to remind them that he'd helped with locations for other productions. He'd also been instrumental in finding some locals to work as extras, and because of this he claimed to be something of a showbiz wiz himself. Gunderson, in short, was tiresome. The three men schemed of ways to get rid of him, asked him for things they didn't think he could procure but would send him away for long intervals. Only he would pop up again a short time later, regardless of whether he'd been successful or not, and the three men had to find other ways to avoid his prodding for stories about certain actors and actresses they'd worked with, and especially about their movie's notoriously reclusive director, under whose auspices they had come to this alpine haunt.

Alone, the three "Hollywood boys" had plenty of stories to tell. Soaking in the hot springs at the opposite end of Main Street, steam weeping off the thermal waters pumped by a conduit of pipes tapped deep into the granite wellsprings, the heat opening their pores and dizzying their brains, they told tales that each knew to be true. "The truth about [this actress] is that she and everybody else mistake looks for talent." "[This director] made a devilish little deal to never make another film so that his proclivity for prepubescent girls would be overlooked." Gradually they fell into meditative silence. Their skins pruned in the water and then dried out in the air, little white flecks of dermis flaking off. They trekked back up Main and in through the stained glass doors of the wet-wood-smelling hotel and into their separate rooms and beds.

The morning air that greeted them was sweet, filtered through the pines and sage and snowmelt. They breathed it in at the top of the street and looked down through the dormant town. The architecture would do: the slope of the street and its ascending construction of Queen Anne and Carpenter Gothic; the red brick courthouse that was almost too perfect for an exterior; and that red-painted livery was just a postcard, leaning like a splintered Tower of Pisa, still sturdy and standing. True, there was not much space—the crew and equipment (lights, cameras, cables) would be squeezed together—but yes, they agreed, they should film here.

They were waiting to see one last location: the setting for the alpine chase between the film's pro- and antagonists. The scene had changed a couple times, the screenwriter still unsatisfied. The original story had focused on one villain, holed up in a saloon, shooting his way out. The new script had a climax with two outlaw brothers and an attempted escape up to the rocky peaks where they must decide: either give up and save each other, or one would sacrifice the other for potential freedom.

Gunderson had promised to set the Hollywood boys up with a certain guide, a man of unreserved repute and adventure. "Yankee Boy Basin will be perfect for your picture," Gunderson said. "Your guide will show you. The man's an ex-trapper." Ex-trapper, hunter, mountain climber, arms the size of aspen trunks. According to Gunderson, this guide drove a snowplow up and down Red Mountain in the winter. He had rescued a party cut off up near the ghost town of Tomboy. He once hit an elk driving the narrow highway one night, an accident that tossed his truck and gave him a broken collarbone and ribs, but he managed with the help of a passing car to strap the elk to the bed and save the meat.

The three men imagined him at bullfights at the festival of San Fermín. They imagined him posing for a photo in front of a trophy rhino head in Khartoum. They imagined the stories he'd share and that they, afterward, would have to tell. The Hollywood boys were sold.

"Say, Gunderson, when are we going to meet this guide?"

"Tomorrow morning," Gunderson wheezed, then dabbed his forehead with his handkerchief.

But Gunderson was sad to report the next morning that the guide was not there; he had been caught up in some business in Ophir, and would not arrive until that night at the earliest, far too late to go up to the Basin. The Hollywood boys looked at their watches. The studio production company and the director, an auteur of the most exacting standards, would be expecting them in two days' time. The three men elected that Gunderson should take them anyway, *sans* guide, drop them off, and pick them up the next day. Gunderson, who seemed especially bloated and red at that early hour, told them he was terribly sorry for the hiccup, but the gentlemen should not be left alone in the wilderness. He would find some other guide, someone who knew the area.

"Better make it fast, Gundy," the screenwriter let slip the nickname they'd given him. Embarrassed, apologetic, Gunderson trundled off into the town to make inquiries, and the three men went back to the hotel bar for an early drink.

An hour later there was a call to the hotel. Gunderson had arranged a new guide, and after a quick lunch just before noon the three men set their minimal gear on the hotel steps and took a long look down the sloping street, where each exited himself with the sense that the earth might crack under their feet, the buildings fall away, and something might grow out of a gaping fissure where the deep-buried steam converging with the cold chalky river. Instead, Gunderson pulled up in an old Jeep. They loaded in and tilted their way up out of town toward the mountain.

The Jeep road, a wagon-rutted path once meant for access to the mine, was pitted and rock-strewn, and the four men bounced over each boulder and hollow. The cliff wall could have dragged its rocky knuckles across the side of the Jeep, so close did Gunderson hug it, but the alternative was slipping off the mountainside and into a chasm of oblivion. Each man gritted his teeth and gripped what he could. Though they did not know it or share it, both Gunderson and the screenwriter silently reflected on rides they'd taken in similar vehicles in humid mountain zones in the last armed conflict, the hard jostles rattling their bodies back to a time when snipers could be waiting around the next rocky crag.

They passed the remains of a mining town, splintered wood structures swept by neglect that betrayed the hardy souls who once built them but now were no more. Rust-colored tailings spilled out of the old mine's orifices. The road wound, crouched beneath a sturdy cliff overhang that, if loosed, would have flattened the men and their rubber-wheeled chassis while the high hillsides looked indifferently on. But the sun was out, the sky blue, the air thin and thinning, and the road eventually widened a bit.

The men all soon became quite jovial. The director of photography began bleating a triumphant war march from a film he'd worked on a couple years before, and soon everyone, even Gunderson with his church-trained baritone, was singing along. They passed a boy with a donkey making their way up the road, and the director of photography stood up and saluted.

The Jeep crawled with its singing crew over small brooks carved out by mountain runoff; it overtook little boulders that had rolled into the path. Gunderson was not a bad driver. Soon enough they'd arrived at the stopping point, where the Jeep could go no further.

It was here that Gunderson would leave them. The guide would take them up the Basin toward the summit. "Lovely wildflowers this time of year," Gunderson added, smiling, obviously pleased with his performance. The three Hollywood boys were pleased, too, and the location manager pulled out a bill and handed it to Gunderson, who refused at first but, seeing it was both expected and acceptable, nodded and thanked them.

Gunderson helped them with their meager gear—the guide was to bring the rest—and then waited with the men at the Jeep. And they waited. And looked to the horizon, and wondered from which direction the guide would come. And looked at watches and smoked cigarettes and wondered if any guide was coming at all. Now a white envelope of cloud appeared over the peak beyond them, the first cloud of the day, and Gunderson could see the men's patience waning and wanted to make clear that his was, too. Until from below they saw the boy with the donkey and stood in silent observation of his approach. He was wearing a wide-brimmed hat that shaded his face and neck, a puffed wool shirt, and wool pants rolled at the cuffs to reveal wool stockings and high shining boots. He held the rope to the donkey's harness delicately, as if to show that the donkey actually needed no harness at all.

And then a revelation: in the bright, clear air they saw that this was not a boy but a girl, or a young lady, somewhere just north or south of twenty. When she lifted her head and the shadow fled they could see her soft face. She was not pretty, but she was much more than plain. She did not smile. She led the donkey to them and, keeping the harness light in her left palm, she held out her right hand to offer a shake.

"Virginia Nelson," she said. She looked each man in the eye, nodded, pressed her lips into a line, said her name, and then moved to the next and did the same.

The men looked at each other and at Gunderson, who seemed vexed, at least as much as his round red face could express vexation. He could only say, "Virginia Nelson," making it the fourth time the name had echoed between them. "Jim Nelson's daughter."

"The daughter of the guide?" the screenwriter asked.

"I'm afraid not." Gunderson shook his head solemnly and removed his hat, as though they were all suddenly attending the man's funeral. With his palm he wiped his forehead, and it was clear that Gunderson had betrayed them.

"My father owns the general store," Virginia Nelson said. Her voice was husky, round and full, despite her small frame. It made her older. There was a confidence and expectancy in that voice, as if she were surprised the men had never heard a name so famous as "Jim Nelson."

Gunderson patted the side of the jeep. "This is when I leave you," he said. "I'll meet you tomorrow at eleven." And, as no one said anything else, he hopped back in the jeep, executed a careful 180, and was soon crawling tail-tucked back down the mountain.

"Well, should we get going?" the location manager asked, trying to seem eager.

Virginia did not move, except to point up to the horizon towering above them. "Storm's coming," she said, and sure enough the single cloud had made some grayer friends.

"A little rain never hurt anyone," the screenwriter said.

But Virginia shook her head and said, "Not rain. Lightning. Killed a hiker on Sneffels last year. If we wait here a bit, the storm will pass. They usually just kick up a little dust."

"Look, Miss," the screenwriter said, widening his legs and flattening his shoulders into a matador's stance, "I don't want to tell you how to do your job here, but I expect Mr. Gunderson must have mentioned that we are interested in this area for a Hollywood production. You know, pictures. You've been to the movies?"

The girl nodded.

"Good. You can imagine there's a lot of money at stake. If we like this area, it means big bucks for your little town here. So we need to like this area. And part of your job, which I think Mr. Gunderson would also have mentioned, is that you need to help us like it. That way we can go back to our studio and say, Yes, let's film there."

"Mr. Gunderson mentioned that," Virginia agreed.

"I thought he would," the screenwriter said. "That's the way it is: we sell stories, you sell us this place." He looked to the director of photography.

The director of photography took up the cue. "We need to be up the mountain this evening. Check the evening light and what have you. Not one of us will mind a little rainstorm."

The screenwriter made a few demonstrable steps forward, ushering the other men to follow. They did. After a few yards they heard their guide behind them tell Liberty—or Freedom (for something like that was the donkey's name)—to gee up. The donkey clopped along and, their point made, the men stepped aside and let Virginia Nelson pass.

The rain came. The clouds billowed and darkened and let fall a few drops, fat ones that splattered like spit on the trail. From out of the ground the rain pulled smells rooted in the origins of the world. It was florid, this smell, filled with earth and rhizome, shoot and leaf, suturing the space where petal met air. The three men had never smelled anything so satisfying. They hiked on, paused, hiked again. Their shoulders and thighs were soaked, Liberty's ears twitched, and the surrounding mountains—castles where long-dead gods might have reigned—looked down on the small bethlehemic procession.

Without warning, lightning popped like a photographer's flash and the thunder rolled instantly down toward them, raising their neck hairs and heart rates. Virginia stopped and said she preferred to wait, that the higher they went toward the ridge, the more dangerous. But see? There, opening up beyond the raincloud, was a slit of blue sky.

The men made faces of displeasure, but now tended to agree, and so each found a rock and sat under his hat and the drizzling sky.

Within thirty minutes the storm had passed and with it any atmospheric memory of a storm. The ground was wet, the grasses were wet, but the sun was back in its too-close brilliance. They took it all in. The director of photography and location manager framed the scene, the screenwriter looked to the peaks for inspiration. He saw the outlaw brothers in his story, one simple but intrinsically good, the other smart but wicked, dashing up along the ridge. Of course, they probably could not film up there, but he felt a sudden compulsion to be up there himself, as high as one could go, looking back down over creation. He had promised the director that the smart, wicked one would win, sacrificing the simple, good one, in order to preserve himself. The wicked one would be caught in the end, having given up his poor dumb brother for nothing. But now the screenwriter was thinking he wanted it the other way around: the simple one would survive, would mourn terribly the loss of his mad brother, never understanding where they went wrong.

They crossed a small stream and on either side a phalanx of wildflowers rose before them. They shimmered, glazed with rain and sun.

"Say, Ginny," the screenwriter said, "give us the names of some flowers here, would you? Would you just look at the columbine. It's columbine, isn't it?"

"Columbine here," Virginia paused, knelt, and brushed a petal with her forefinger. She rose. "Paintbrush, different colors: pink there, orange there."

The men looked at each other as she methodically pointed them out.

"Bluebells. The yellow ones there are little sunflowers. At least what I've heard them called."

It was dazzling, these meadows of flowers. Even the screenwriter got out his little snap camera to bend in close and take a few photos.

Bees buzzed among the bluebells, paused and let their legs wick with pollen. A couple of monarch butterflies chased each other like paramours. "Look," the director of photography pointed them out to the screenwriter. "It's you and what's-her-name."

The screenwriter made a *humph* sound but did not disagree.

"Those white clusters," the location manager said to Virginia. "Cardamine?"

"Bittercress," she corrected. She said it so flatly that it seemed she left off a "Sir."

"Yes," he said. "Bittercress is cardamine."

"If you say so. I only know bittercress."

"We should keep moving," the director of photography said, taking off again. He began to think out loud: the logistics of getting a crew up there, even a small one. The equipment.

"But the *authenticity*," the screenwriter stressed. "*This* is what I envisioned." And indeed he could not help but imagine himself, impossible as it was, leaping from mountaintop to mountaintop.

By now the air had cooled some from the rain, but the sun was searing. The men were easily winded and needed frequent breaks for water, which Liberty carried and Virginia stopped and procured for them each time they requested it, waiting until they'd swallowed and then systematically placing it back into Liberty's load.

"Is it your donkey?" the screenwriter asked.

"My father's," Virginia replied.

"Jim's his name, isn't it?" the director of photography said and raised his eyebrows to the screenwriter. "Your father, not the donkey." The screenwriter caught the look.

Virginia said, "Yes."

"Must be isolating," the screenwriter said, as if to no one, or as if to the mountains themselves, who were so large they would not deign to hear him if they could. But in the ensuing silence it was clear he had expected Virginia to respond. "Isolating," he repeated. "What's it like growing up here, Ginny?"

"I didn't," Virginia said.

"But your father runs the general store," the location manager said.

"We moved from Grand Junction two years ago," Virginia said.

The location manager sighed.

"This is his third store," Virginia said. "The one in Grand Junction, one in Montrose, and the one here."

"So you are what," the screenwriter said, "a kind of general store heiress? Your father going to be going national soon?"

The men smiled at each other.

"He doesn't involve me in those decisions," she said.

This prompted even greater grins.

"You do much of this?" the screenwriter said. "Guiding, I mean?"

"Once before," Virginia said.

"Just the once, huh? And what got a pretty lady like you into mountaineering?"

"Well, I love the mountains, sir. Always did. I told my father we should start up an outfitting business as a service at the store. He said, 'You do it.' So I saved up and bought Liberty here."

"That's it? Just up and decided?"

"Yes, sir."

They trucked on. Step after step. They were well above treeline now. The unobstructed carpet of the world continued to spread before them until, after an hour or so, they were just below the top.

"I'll set up camp here," Virginia said, slowing Liberty to a halt. "Over that ridge there"—she nodded up ahead of them—"there's a little lake. Maybe you want to take a look while I get us settled."

"Is this the best spot?" the location manger asked. "Maybe nearer the peak?"

Virginia began to unbuckle the gear from Liberty's back. "It's the last bit of level ground."

"You sure you don't need our help, Ginny?" the screenwriter winked.

"No, thank you," she replied.

"All right, men," the director of photography said, "to the lake!" He began a high march step, which the others did not imitate.

It was another twenty minutes to the ridge. From there they were almost truly at the top. The peaks mounded before them, no longer looming giants but equals.

Just a short way below them on the other side stood a mountain lake, and they scurried down like boys running for the ocean. They took off their boots and socks and dipped their feet in the frigid water. They walked barefoot on the surrounding scree, balancing like tightrope walkers on the rocks piercing the balls of their feet. They leapt barefoot into a nearby snowfield, made snowballs and threw them at each other, mostly missing. The location manager lost his balance and fell backwards, then made a show of it and swept his arms and legs to form a snow angel.

By the time they got their boots back on they were fairly chilled.

"We should make a nice, big campfire," the location manager said. The others agreed. Reaching the top of the ridge, they looked down to see a beetle-sized Liberty standing beside two tents, one large, one small.

"A magnificent beast," the director of photography remarked.

"And the donkey isn't bad either," the location manager said.

The men had a chuckle and watched Virginia duck out of the smaller tent.

"Not the most charming lass," the director of photography said.

"Ass?" corrected the location manager.

"A goddamn know-it-all," said the screenwriter.

"Or thinks she is," said the location manager.

"Thanks for nothin', Gundy," the screenwriter smirked, and each man felt acutely that they were all in the wrong adventure story.

"Gunderson!" the location manager shouted across the mountaintops and Basin. The other two called out, "Gun-der-son!" until it was a small chorus of "Gunder-sons" reverberating through the hills, their voices echoing down to their guide, so small below.

Back at camp, Virginia pointed out the larger tent, where sleeping bags had been rolled out, three in a row. The men took their belongings inside. It was now significantly cooler on the mountain, and they put on jackets.

"Say, Miss Nelson, let's build us a campfire," the location manager said, emerging from the tent and rubbing his hands together.

"The land is private property," Virginia replied. "We can't have a fire."

"Who's going to know?" the director of photography said from inside the tent.

"There's no wood," Virginia countered, "unless you go back down."

The director of photography came out and had a look for himself. True, there was very little one could use as kindling.

The screenwriter joined them outside. "Those old mine ruins," he said. "There are some splinters there we could use."

"The mine is private, too."

The screenwriter drew his mouth into a terse expression. He unbuttoned the top three buttons of his jacket and pulled one aside to reveal the handle of a revolver. "I fear neither man nor beast," he said.

"Please don't fire that here," Virginia frowned.

"I'll hunt our dinner," the screenwriter said.

"Somebody hears shooting, they might come up," Virginia said. "It's private property…"

"We will defend our territory!" the location manager shouted militantly and saluted. Liberty took a step backward. "Fear not, my trusty steed!" the location manager consoled. The men laughed but Virginia and Liberty did not.

"OK, Ginny," the screenwriter chuckled and buttoned up his jacket to show he'd secured his weapon. "But iffin' they come fer us, yuh can rest yer head knowin' I'd protect yuh."

Virginia cooked stew on a bright green Coleman stove. The men slapped at mosquitoes. The screenwriter poured the other two each a healthy dram of the Scotch he'd had the bartender load. He raised the flagon to Virginia at her stove but she shook her head no. He took a swig. "Suit yourself, Ironsides," he muttered to himself behind the up-kipped flask.

Evening was a thick gray, swiftly turning to night. They ate out of tin bowls, discussed some technical aspects of filming in this location, especially concerns about light and weather. But imagine those wildflowers on the screen!

"They'll be gone in a couple weeks," Virginia said. "Wildflower season is short, and you're wanting to film in September."

They looked at her. "Well, then, forget the flowers," the director of photography sneered.

She gave them a single lantern and took one for herself and the smaller tent. She got Liberty fed and watered and settled for the night.

Alone at last, the men sat outside, smoking and chatting.

"If we're outta Scotch, I'm gonna lose my temper," the screenwriter said.

The location manager went into their tent and brought out a bottle that he'd pinched from the hotel.

"Santa Maria!" the director of photography said. "A miracle!"

"It keeps you warm until it doesn't," the location manager said.

They fell silent. Breathed the crisp air. Felt the burn in their veins, in their heads, and the coldness in their asses.

"I've traveled to the base of Kilimanjaro," the screenwriter began out of nowhere, "where it is said a spirit cat haunts the mountain." His face was completely obscured by the dark.

"Are we telling ghost stories?" the director of photography said.

"I have visited mountain villages in Austria," the screenwriter intoned, "where certain mythical monsters, Bigfoot types with horns and hooves who stand upright like a man, come at Christmas with St. Nicholas, and beat the children."

"Some Christmas," the location manager lamented.

"*I'm dreaming of a white Christmas*," the director of photography crooned.

"Shhh," said the screenwriter.

The location manager harmonized in counter-tenor: "*Just like the ones I used to know.*"

"Shhh!" The screenwriter stood and walked a few paces away, then turned and whisper-whistled for his companions to join him.

"I'm wondering," he said conspiratorially. "What if we had a little fun with little Lady Ironsides?"

They all looked over the Virginia Nelson's tent, its outline vague in the gloaming.

"What are we talking about?"

"Nothing much. Just a scare. Good for a laugh."

"I don't know."

"Some excitement, a story to tell tomorrow. Don't you think we deserve a story?"

And he told them his plan.

After loudly enunciated *Good nights*, they climbed into their tent, drunkenly rearranged the sleeping bags head to foot, got in them, and were swallowed by the silence. It was profound. Nothing seemed to stir, and they quickly tuned their ears to the sound of their own breathing and the heartbeats in their heads.

Not a few minutes later the director of photography was roused from near sleep. The screenwriter's voice was low, and because the director of photography's ears rang when he was stewed, he had a hard time making out the words. It was more like gestures given to a squad column. They carefully undid the flap and moved out.

The stars spun above, Scotch-blurred. It was a sloshing struggle, but director of photography scrambled up the slope to a position about fifty feet above their camp. The location manager remained by the men's tent, and the screenwriter crept over to Virginia's. Stage set, each man in place.

First came the overture. The director of photography began to bray, moving then between something of a low moo and a grunt. He started softly, working his way up into a snarl and snorting that once or twice make him choke. After a reasonable introduction to the theme, he lifted one leg, then the next, and stomped slowly toward the tents, growing louder with each footfall, alternately raising his arms and beating his chest.

Liberty awoke and twitched his ears, swayed his head back and forth. The screenwriter held up his hand to sternly warn the donkey not to ruin this.

The symphony begun, it was time to bring in the other instruments. The location manager, with a bit of vibrato, chimed, "Say, fellas, you hear something? Fellas? What's that noise?"

Snarling and stomping crescendo.

"Fellas, something's out there! Something's coming this way!"

An unearthly yowl. Liberty's uncomfortable hoofclops and the sound of straining tether.

Followed by a bit of improvisation: "It's coming for us! Get the gun!"

Eruption in climatic action as the director of photography roared, the location manager screamed, and the screenwriter howled and violently shook Virginia Nelson's tent. It was terrific, the shaking, meant to frighten her, to do something more, to raise her to inhuman terror. But nothing moved within.

The screenwriter took the silence as a sign to up the ante even further, and so he began slapping and kicking the canvas wall. "God damn it Ginny! Wake up!" When there was still no sound, he took two steps back, slipped out his revolver and fired it once into the air.

The gunshot sent Liberty slipping on the loose stone under his hooves. The director of photography and location manager froze, covering their ears in fear that another might go off. In the echo of the report the screenwriter still furiously shook Virginia Nelson's tent poles, snarling, "Oh the things I'm gonna do to you, missy! Oh the things!"

"OK! OK!" the director of photography hollered. "Woah there! Hold up!"

The screenwriter gave the tent one last slap and stepped back, panting. Inside nothing stirred.

"Hey girlie! Hey Ginny!" he shouted. "I said wake up! It's a goddamn joke!"

Silence. The men waited, their hearts thundering.

"What the hell?" the location manager said. "Is she really asleep?"

The screenwriter stepped to Liberty and grabbed the donkey's harness, giving it a jerk so that the animal brayed. The next sound was the cocking of the gun. "I'm gonna stick this gun right up your ass's ass!"

"Jeez!" the location manager wheezed. "Hold on now!"

The screenwriter positioned the revolver next to Liberty's temple. "Let's eat us some donkey."

"Knock it off!" the director of photography hissed.

Stones clacking from up behind him drew the director of photography's attention upslope, where a large tree stood. It was out of place. He knew there was no tree there. He watched to see if it would move, make itself known. Enough booze had sweated out of him to quickly realize that the shape was in fact Virginia Nelson, watching, audience to the entire spectacle.

"Bang," the screenwriter said. He pushed away Liberty's face and took a slippery step backwards, fumbling the gun. A shot exploded and echoed across the hills.

"God *damn*! I've fucking shot myself!"

For an instant the reality of the moment failed to fully exert itself. When it did, the other two stumbled to the screenwriter's aid.

"God damn! Oh God damn!"

"How bad is it?" said the director of photography.

"I can't see a thing!" the location manager said.

"Mary Jesus motherfuck!" the screenwriter belted. "Oh, God damn, God damn!"

"Get a flashlight!" said the director of photography.

"Where? Where?" The location manager ran back to their tent and started tearing it apart.

"I'm gonna fucking die here," said the screenwriter.

"You're not gonna die."

"How do you know?"

The director of photography did not know, so he did not say anything.

The flashlight beam was on them. At the other end was Virginia Nelson. She handed the flashlight to the director of photography and began unbuttoning her shirt. The director of photography shone the light on her, then realized he was doing so and turned the light back on the screenwriter. He'd seen enough to know that she was wearing a sleeveless undershirt, and that she looked rather lovely beneath her flannel. He pointed the flashlight down the screenwriter's leg and there, on the shin, gleamed a terrible red spot. A little lower he saw pooling blood on the ground. The location manager emerged running from the tent empty-handed, clasped his hands to his mouth when he saw the blood.

"Ah jeez! Jeez!"

Virginia Nelson wrapped her shirt tightly around the wound.

"Will that work?" the location manager trembled. "Shouldn't we make a tourniquet or something?"

"Hold this tight to his leg," Virginia said.

"I'll faint."

"Give it here," the director of photography said. He handed the location manager the flashlight as Virginia picked up the revolver and set it off in the darkness.

Out of the corner of his eye the director of photography thought he glimpsed lightning. He turned to see two bright eyes of a vehicle crawling up the mountain toward them.

"God damn," the screenwriter moaned.

"Look at that," the director of photography said. The location manager saw it too, and shone the flashlight down toward the headlights and clicked it off and on, off and on.

"It's OK, Charlie," the location manager said. "Somebody's coming. We'll get you down to a hospital. Oh, I gotta sit down."

"Get some blankets," Virginia said. The location manager complied and Virginia rolled one into a pillow and put the other one over the screenwriter.

"God," the screenwriter said. "God."

"Ah, shit, Charlie," the location manager said. He was beginning to cry.

"Shine that light down there," the director of photography said.

They watched the headlights grow larger, heading up the hill. Had it been five minutes or an hour when they at last pulled up?

The Jeep idled. Liberty kicked the ground nervously. The director of photography raised his right hand in a wave.

Both Jeep doors opened, first one then the other, and two men got out. Their faces were indiscernible behind the bright headlights, but their shadowed figures loomed large.

"Thank God you're here!" the location manager squeaked. "Our friend's been shot!"

"Heard a shot," one of the large dark men said. He was deep voiced, calm.

"He needs a hospital," the director of photography said.

"A lot of shooting goin' on up here tonight," said the dark man's voice.

"Will you take our friend back to town?" the location manager said. "He needs a doctor." He looked down to the screenwriter, whose eyes were open and whose mouth was moving slightly, though no sound was coming from it.

"'S private property," the dark man said.

"What's the girl doing here?" his companion said. His voice was higher, younger sounding.

His question drew the first, larger man's attention to Virginia. "You fellas up to some sick shit?"

"Our guide!" blurted the location manager. "She's our guide!"

"We're from Los Angeles, sir," the director of photography said, his hands stuck to the bloody wrapped wound. His bladder was completely full and he was sure he was about to douse his pants. "Here for a movie shoot. Our friend…"

"Movie?" said the first man.

"A movie. We're here to make a movie," said the location manager.

"Sounds like some sick shit," said the younger-sounding man.

"How about it, girlie?" the first man said. "You from Hollywood? You making a movie with these boys?"

They waited for Virginia to speak. When she did, she said, "I'm their guide, sir. Jim Nelson's daughter. Of Nelson's General Store."

An age seemed to pass during which no one said anything.

"Shouldn't be up here alone with a buncha men," the younger-voiced one muttered at last. "Porno or something.'"

"You up to some sinful shit up here?" the first man said.

"Sir," the director of photography began. "Our real guide was unable to…"

"Get in," the first man cut him off and shifted forward so that a headlight caught his form. He was bearded, barrel-bellied. Big Foot.

"Oh, thank God," the location manager said. "Our friend's in shock. I think he's in shock!"

"Not him," the big man said. "Her."

"You can't…" the location manager started, but thought again.

"I said, get in."

No one moved. The Jeep engine rattled and resumed its hum. The younger-voiced man took a step sideways.

"The man was drunk," Virginia Nelson panted. "He was waving his firearm. He threatened my donkey. He shot once, but was drunk enough he missed. These men wrestled the gun from him, handed it to me while they tried to subdue him. He broke free and then started for me. I shot him. I shot him in the leg."

The location manager let go a sob.

"That so?" the big man said.

Virginia Nelson nodded.

"You're the guide?"

"Yes, sir."

"Where's the gun?" the big man said.

Virginia looked about but did not move.

"Fetch it."

Virginia crossed over to the spot where she thought she'd placed the gun. She found it by its glint, lifted it loosely by the handle.

"C'mere," the big man said. "Into the light."

Virginia stepped back into the glare.

"Hold it up," the big man said.

Virginia lifted it.

"Point it like you did," the big man said. "At him there, on the ground. Like you did when you shot him."

Virginia pointed it to where the screenwriter lay. The Jeep coughed. The night was a purple bruise.

"There," the big man said. "Just like that. That's better."

KIMBERLY KRUGE

In-Migration

Today I have to prove I married for love;
so I'll use the word *love*
as if it were consistently defined—
and I'll use the word *happy*
as if it were a state of being.

I don't want to get too heady
with the official,
ponytailed and clean-faced.
This is about keeping my mouth shut.

But she isn't unlikeable—
her flag on her sleeve—
and before I know it,
I am telling her
I hate long lines and franchises,
and how I used to dye my hair dark,
and how I monitor the movements
of a nearby volcano,
and I am about to tell her
about the Yerbabuena, the town at its base,
where a woman told me the volcano shrouds itself
from me, embarrassed to show a stranger
its supposed deadliness, its nature.

I am about to tell her I earn under the table,
and that I've
failed at immigration and
failed at love before
and that it's a stupid question,
if I am happy,
and that who knows what
love is anyways,

and wouldn't she agree
—she isn't unlikeable—
the woman with a newborn
who yells like a warrior
through the night in
the outskirts of the city
where she lives,
where people still walk to get around.

But I hold my tongue between my teeth,
like the beginning and ending of so many things.

And as she types into a format letter
my name and date of birth,
the dates of my in- and out-migrations,
my reasons for both,
and that I am to *dedicate myself to the home now,*
and *make poems with the intention to publish,*
and that *someone is required to care for me,*
and that I've submitted, as evidence
of the *existence of love and contentment,*
photos of me and my husband,

I realize how true it all reads.
She's taken my head out of it.
She's made it into a proof with tight laws.

I look out at our city
basked in terrible midday yellow.
It is falling down. It is badly made.
Manic and, then, mad.

On the in-side of the window—
a plastic appliqué of a tree
and the image of children printed on paper,
a uniform on the rack held
as if a body were in it.

STEPHANIE ROGERS

Fat Girl Ghazal

At the bar, I ran into a frat boy who called me a fat girl.
He said, "No one wants to sleep with a fucking fat girl."

I opened my thighs, joked with him, "Pretty please?"
Later, I mascara-wrecked my pillow, a crying fat girl.

Once, a homeless man freaked out when I ignored him.
He yelled, "Move, you stupid bitch, you fucking fat girl."

I won't lie. I called my sister while sobbing on the toilet.
She said, "What is *wrong* with people?" I said, "Fat girls?"

My boyfriend says he loves my waves of flab, my breasts.
All his exes: skinny. Is he just pretending to like a fat girl?

Get over yourself, I tell myself in mirrors, in reflections.
Because! I'm tired of playing the funny one, the fat girl.

A driver screamed, "Get your fat ass out of the street."
I looked down, picked up my pace, ashamed, a fat girl.

I suck in my stomach, pull back my shoulders, envious:
the blondes who ride my block on bikes aren't fat girls.

Some days, I accidentally heave my weight in public.
People stare, "Don't sit there. Oh shit, another fat girl."

I'm taught to either love my body, hate it, love it, hate it.
Even friends think, "Steph, you're pretty! (for a fat girl)."

DAVID McLOGHLIN

Dendrochronology

I live underneath the scriptorium.
I perceive sunlight hear birdsong
through him   in him.

He is the only aperture.
I am an epoch in microfiche
hair on a fiddlehead

its genital stem—*f* uncoiling
in time lapse in the margin
of his lectern. I can't be touched

by sundials   or the shadows
from the markers of history.
I am unleavened

dissolving in his mouth.
I live under a fern curlicue.
In the word forest   I am less

than the faintest tree ring.
From the room under the room
walled-in inside him I hear

the First Years the new boys
and him like a prophet
going out to walk among them.

ELLEN DORÉ WATSON

March 31st and the frogs

are going nutso down in that sinkhole
pond. Sounds like a cauldron on high
happy boil. I'm not there yet, you're
nonexistent, my roommates are sins.
All that I read confirms darkness—who
asked poems to be lugubrious chariots
to the pitch? It's safe, though, living
in paper rooms with words arriving
oh yes like bullets, expected, or like
manatees—wonder underwater.
Those actual frogs are nothing but
out there, with their three-chambered
non-human hearts, their skin cleaning
the air we share, and they could care
less whether I thank or curse them
for their farty calls speaking sex.

MARGARET CIPRIANO

Modern Survival

In the summer of identifying dangerous things,
the father takes his daughter
to see a wasp nest under slatted shutters.
With a broom, he beats their buzzing house
and the daughter swells up. *Collateral damage,*
he says. *Bad things can always hurt you back.*
It is the same for the poison
ivy, the rashes that crawl
up their arms and turn their skin inside
out. But always, the need for weeding.
When all the light bulbs break,
the daughter asks the father
if the world still wants them in it.
Grab a shovel, says the father.
And in sunlight and moonlight they turn
the earth up. They are making
a new house, and here, the father thinks,
nothing can hurt them. When it rains,
they sleep on their backs and get mud
in their mouths. Soon, the father forgets
about the daughter. He is in love
with the shovel. He strokes its metal
edge. He is so thankful to be saved.
The daughter never stops looking up.

ANALICIA SOTELO

My Mother as the Face of God

For now, we are both alive.

Another Sunday afternoon: I'm looking out
your bedroom window, looking down

at the cars speeding like stars in daylight

as you imagine they'll asteroid
right through our wooden fence,

burn up the roses you carefully planted;
the ones that stand delicately

as if for a picture
where someone is missing from the family reunion,
but no one wants to talk about it.

This is eternity.
I make fun of your children's garden:

a wrought iron table with matching chairs,
a bronze rabbit, curious as taxidermy,
a tea set without tea.

I think I just saw
one of your ghost children
running around out there, I say.

I'm morbid and loving. You made me.

You pay bills on a quilted blanket
while I picture them—their eyes

flashing, their cheeks—a dark, daguerreotype silver,
their mouths—accidental knife marks on a paper plate.

Mother, your likeness is not easy
or accidental. I am trying to understand it, trying

to become the opening
your light projects painfully through.

Trauma with Haberdashery

Even now at the sea wall:

I see the foam,
I see the bird's bones and feathers,
the mite-infested corset,
and what do I do?

I put on airs, stare too long
while the insects fatten up for the occasion.

I hold my breath
I pose as if willing
to be ripped apart from the amygdala.

You make me feel I'm falling
into a ravine with children
dressed in felt flames.

Look at their chalkboard cheeks.
They're marked forever.

I am not saying I was marked,
I am saying I could have been and that is
stage-worthy trauma.

I touch my ribbons.
I think of you saying: *You're charming*
with your anachronistic appetite

like a button that becomes a bird's eye on the sand

in this the 21st century
where men still love girls, but rarely admit it,
and history binds you to your signature.

ROBERT ARCHAMBEAU

Reggie Watts and Karl Pilkington Wrestle in Heaven

THEY DON'T WRESTLE, AND THEY aren't in Heaven, but it's a better title than "The Wind and the Lion, or: Reggie Watts and Karl Pilkington, an Essay That Gets a Little Dark and Political at the End."

•

AT THE END of *The Wind and the Lion*, a mid-seventies orientalist extravaganza of a film, a Barbary pirate king played by Sean Connery writes to a distant Teddy Roosevelt, whose warships and Marines—representatives of modernity and the budding American empire—threaten to destroy him and his people. "I, like the lion, must stay in my place," intones Connery in voiceover, not quite managing to get the Scotland out of his voice, "while you, like the wind, will never know yours."

•

THERE ARE MANY ways to understand comedy. There's Hobbes' way, which is all about feeling superior to the schmuck who took a pie to the face; Kant's way, which is about the unexpectedness of using a pie as a projectile; and Freud's, which says we're just giggling with relief when we stop suppressing our forbidden aggressions and smash a pie into some fool's face. But if you want to understand two of the most striking figures of contemporary comedy, Reggie Watts and Karl Pilkington, you could do worse than to start with the words of a fictional Barbary pirate.

To be clear: Pilkington's the lion in this scenario. The bald, Mancunian lion. And Reggie Watts, whose voluminous afro differentiates him from Pilkington as much as his apparent cosmopolitan placelessness, is the wind. Let's start with the lion.

•

EVERYONE WHO STUMBLED through graduate school in the humanities knows Kant credited David Hume with awakening him from his dogmatic slumber, but few know that he cribbed from another Scottish philosopher, James Beattie, when he put together his theory of the comic as the incongruous. Laughter, Beattie says, arises when things that don't belong together unite—and Kant said much the same, more prominently and with far less clarity. And incongruity does explain a great deal of comedy, from Steve Martin wearing an arrow through his head while playing banjo in old *Saturday Night Live* episodes, to any solemn cleric or public speaker letting loose with a burst of surprisingly audible flatulence. It would seem to explain much of the comic effect of watching Karl Pilkington travel the world in the Sky TV series *An Idiot Abroad*. When, for example, Karl Pilkington stands on the Great Wall of China, looking out over the vast, venerable, and sublime fortification as it snakes away over the mountains of the Chinese north, we'd expect something like awe from him. He even seems, for a moment, to provide it, saying "It goes on for miles, over hills and such," before deflating it all: "but so does the M6" (a perpetually traffic-clogged British motorway). The reaction is incongruous in a way Beattie and Kant would understand. And it involves something like the special kind of incongruity Mikhail Bakhtin saw as central to comedy—the "transcoding" in which something grand or sacred is juxtaposed to something banal or (in the most powerful cases) obscene. But if we understand Karl Pilkington merely as a producer of incongruous comments, we miss what's special to him. We miss what makes him a lion.

•

YOU WANT TO understand Karl Pilkington? Then you want to understand the power of narrowness. You want to understand the brilliance of narrowness.

It was Ricky Gervais, who produced and hosted *An Idiot Abroad*, who designated Pilkington as the titular idiot. Indeed, he labored, in the first episode, to get at the exact nature of Pilkington's putative idiocy. "I don't know the politically correct term," says Gervais, brow furrowed, "A moron? He is a round, empty-headed chimp-like Manc moron... a buffoon." But Gervais couldn't be more wrong. His collaborator and co-host, Stephen Merchant, comes closer to the truth when he calls Pilkington "a typical Little Englander," a man who prefers things as they are at home, and ignores the larger world. The Little Englander takes a narrow view of things, and it's narrowness, not idiocy, which conditions Pilkington's perceptions.

Narrowness, we might remember, was much sought after by artists at the peak moment of Western painting. It was in quest of narrowness that they first built the *camera obscura*; the pinhole that makes the panorama possible.

•

IF MERCHANT SEES more clearly than Gervais the special nature of Pilkington's perceptions, he fails to understand the durability of Pilkington's narrowness. Indeed, he hopes that sending Pilkington around the world to gaze on various historical and architectural wonders will put an end to that narrowness. "The experience of other cultures will change his outlook on the world," says Merchant, "I truly believe travel broadens the mind." But Pilkington's narrowness withstands all assaults. His way of viewing the world is unshakable, and—in Egypt, in Jordan, in Mexico and India, and Brazil—remains utterly unchanged. But what is this point of view? It's the view of working class Manchester where Pilkington grew up. No matter what he sees, no matter how grand or exotic or vast or uplifting the phenomenon, Pilkington sees it in the context of a Mancunian housing estate.

Consider Christ the Redeemer, the enormous, dramatic statue of Jesus set high on a mountain, with Rio de Janeiro sprawling below it, between the mountains and the sea. Pilkington takes one look at the grand, art deco monument, stretching 100 feet above him and thinks on what it could all mean. Finally, in full sincerity, he says "it's like a big ornament—like something Aunt Nora would have next to the telly." And he's right, he's *brilliantly* right. It *is* like a scaled-up ornament Aunt Nora would keep by the telly. Without premeditation, he's deflated something sacred, in the manner described by Bakhtin. And he's made the incongruous—Aunt Nora's telly and the most sacred of Latin American monuments—connect. He hasn't done it in accord with the dictates of Surrealism, which demanded this kind of thing of its poets. He's done it because of his relentless narrowness, the fact that he can't voyage out and embrace new perspectives. No matter where he is, he sees only from the perspective his home place.

That's how he's like the lion. He might be in Rio, but he stays in his place.

•

WILLIAM BLAKE, SAID T. S. Eliot, saw everything "from the center of his own crystal." There was "nothing of the superior person about him"—and this, Eliot continued, "makes him terrifying." Pilkington certainly sees everything from the center of his own crystal, and has nothing of the superior person about him. But is he terrifying? We'll leave that question for the end.

•

YOU LOOK FOR this rootedness, or centeredness, of Pilkington's, and you see it everywhere.

Consider the Treasury Building, the most impressive structure in Petra. Carved by Romans into the rock wall of a strange valley in what is now Jordan, the Treasury is a true marvel of both history and architecture. Shown a photo of the place, Karl Pilkington struggles to understand why such a building would be constructed. Then it comes to him: "it's like cladding" (we would say "siding") "for a cave." You know: a kind of home improvement project. But, continues Karl,

> You be better to be in the cave across from it, where you're looking at it. You're getting the nice view. The people living in it are looking at my hole. I always think that about nice homes and stuff: living there, you're looking at the Council block across the road, they're looking at the nice view.

He goes on, wondering if perhaps the interiors of the grandest structure of Petra may be deficient. "If I'm an estate agent, you'll say to me, there's a reason it hasn't sold yet—the inside's not that good." Travel broadens the mind, Stephen Merchant says, citing an old bromide. But not Pilkington's mind. He sees structures as he has always seen structures. He sees them as things in need, perhaps of a bit of paint or new boiler. He sees them as places Aunt Nora might put her ornaments and telly.

And here's where Gervais is right in calling the show *An Idiot Abroad*: Karl Pilkington, for all of his brilliance, is, after all, an idiot. Not in the sense of being a moron, or an empty-headed chimp-like buffoon, but in the original Greek sense of idiocy. The ἰδιώτης, or *idiōtēs* was, to the ancient Greeks, simply a person concerned only with his or her private affairs. Like Pilkington, the Greek ἰδιώτης keeps to his own world, his own perspective. Like the lion, he stays in his place..

•

IN HIS GREAT study of laughter, the philosopher Henri Bergson tells us that rigidity is the essence of comedy. Incongruity is funny only because it highlights rigidity of one kind or another: the public speaker's flatulence underlines the rigid formality of the occasion of public speech, and the unbending dictates of the flesh over our will. We could say laughter is a way of policing ourselves against excessive rigidity of body or of mind. We seek, Bergson says, an ideal of flexibility and adaptability, and the pratfall, the imitable-because-predictable mannerism, the literal-minded, are laughable to us because at some level we seek to mark them as expressions of an undesirable rigidity. We want to enforce the kind of flexibility we think of as necessary to life by demeaning the rigid—which is exactly what Stephen Merchant and Ricky Gervais do when they meet with Karl Pilkington for a post-show wrap-up.

We see this when Stephen Merchant sits Pilkington down and confronts him about his meeting with a Brazilian female impersonator. Pilkington had met the man in his masculine street wear and had no idea about his profession. So when the man comes out after changing into feminine clothing and makeup, Pilkington is taken by surprise, and says it's like the man pulled a Worzel Gummidge (Worzel Gummidge was a character in British children's television and literature—a scarecrow who could change heads). Reflecting on this instance, Merchant asks Pilkington:

> Why were you referring to Worzel Gummidge? Why do you make no effort to speak to people in terms they might understand? What's the chance of some guy in Brazil knowing who Worzel Gummidge is? There's people watching this who won't remember who Worzel Gummidge is!

The question isn't so much a question as a harangue, a scolding of Pilkington for the very narrowness and rigidity of perspective that constitutes the rocket fuel powering the show's comedy. I like to imagine that Pilkington replied by saying "Because I, like the lion, must stay in my place," perhaps in Sean Connery's accent and the robes of a Barbary pirate chief.

•

THE FIRST TIME I saw Reggie Watts perform on television, I was so utterly bewildered I couldn't even decide whether the question I needed answered was "what kind of thing am I seeing?" or "what kind of person is this?" It was on Conan O'Brien's show, and it seemed to be a challenge even for his relatively hip late night audience. Watts stood there, an African-American man with a wild afro and a nerdish sweatshirt, and played music on a small sound mixer, looping his own vocal tracks into complex rhythms and singing over it—sometimes gibberish, sometimes scat jazz, sometimes soul. He then started to speak, first in one accent, then another. Each time I thought I was finally seeing the big reveal, that the man who had seemed Jamaican was actually English, or an inner-city African-American, or... well, the ground kept shifting. Was it comedy? A lecture on ethnomusicology? A deliberate attempt to keep pulling the rug out from under the viewer? This last option—Watts likes to call himself a "disin-formationist"—came closest to the truth. None of the "revelations" about who this man *really* was, what he was *really* doing, was a revelation at all: it was just a further metamorphosis. No dance of the seven veils, this act, but a perpetual transmogrifi-cation machine.

The opening of Reggie Watts' television special *Why Shit So Crazy?* serves as a kind of poetics of Watts' metamorphoses. We open on Watts and a group of actors playing his friends as they sit in a 1970s wood-paneled basement, playing some sort of role-playing game, the rules of which are in dispute. Both the fact of the game and the disputed rules matter: what we're about to see, in the program that follows, will be Watts assuming a variety of different roles (beat boxer, rapper, ska singer, stand up comic, faux lecturer, parodist, Ebonics speaker, Englishman, and so forth); and we will see him continually bend or break the rules of performance he sets for himself, and the contexts for interpretation he sets for his audience.

The transformations begin as soon as the role-playing game scene ends. Reggie gets up from the game table, walks out a door, and suddenly stands in a featureless space, the wind blowing back his ample hair as he looks up at a booming voice—a god or demon—that speaks to him from above. But this lasts for only a moment before he turns and, speaking in a perfect English accent, accepts a microphone offered by a formally dressed woman, who whispers in his ear, "Have a good show," pausing a moment before she adds, "your life depends upon it." What are the rules of this world? Are we in a nerd's basement? Are we speaking to a god? Has the staged world ended at last, so that we can see Watts *in propria persona* as he accepts the microphone to take the stage? No! Wait! We're in some kind of *Hunger Games* of comedy, right? No revelation is at hand, though. The rules keep changing, and won't let up until the credits roll.

When Watts does allow the same rules to stay in effect for an extended period of time, it is often to perform a kind of pastiche, in which he "does" the style of one or another kind of person or performer, with most or all of the content one typically finds in such an act vacuumed out, leaving only a hollow shell. Here, for example, is Watts pastiching the kind of stand-up one finds in the world of the Def Comedy Jam:

> Lotta motherfuckers don't know why shit be goin' wrong and shit in the world, you know—how you be reading the news and shit and bad shit be happening all the time, good shit be happenin' like 10% of the time but the rest of the shit all bad and shit you know what I'm saying, motherfucker, know what I'm saying and shit? You all know what I'm saying, yeah, my problem, you know, people so different, people so *different*, motherfuckers like men and women and shit, you know what I'm saying, like *mens* and shit and *womens* know what I'm saying? Girls, like girls be crazy and shit—now let me set this up. Now this is why there be so many problems between the *womens* and the *miz-nens*, aight? Like the womens and shit they be like, "Amo do this shit over here,' you know what I'm saying? Motherfucked up—you gotta change that shit, you know? No *wonder* men think you crazy—and men you too, man, you ain't getting off scot free, know what I'm sayin', you be like 'Ahtingahmondruh do this thing over here.' How you expect to get respect from women when you be doing *that* shit?

The content-free gibberish ("Ahtingahmondruh") at the point that might be the punch-line is just an extreme version of the syntax that delays meaning and the gestures that signal a recognizable form of comedy and a familiar type of speaker without delivering denotative significance. We're reminded that there is a specific kind of African-American comedic delivery that we usually know what to do with—but we're not given enough content to do anything but be reminded of the existence of the genre. The real message, I suppose, is that in this era of media saturation, we all have many familiar interpretive frames, but that we shouldn't get too locked in to applying them when we pick up signals ("motherfuckers," "know what I'm saying?" "womens," "miz-nens") to do so.

•

IF YOU'VE READ the poetry of John Ashbery, you'll understand exactly what's happening in the opening speech from *Spatial*, another of Watts' comedy specials. Here, we begin with ominous music, and Watts emerges on stage, concealed in dark robes, no facial features visible except for what appears to be a single, glowing eye. It's not a very Ashberrian image, but listen to the tone and syntax as they glide around:

> The vestibule has been opened, and all of us continue to act as though nothing will occur. The intergalactic council wishes you to know that all dangers are being dealt with in all quadrants. I know many of you… and some of you I do not, but at some point you will know someone who has met me, and at that point we will be vaguely acquainted. The Telorians would have you believe you are weak, that you are made of nothing, that there is nothing worth fighting for, that you have already lost. But I guarantee you that this can be no further from the truth than from the centers of Andromeda, to the black hole of the Vega system. These weapons shipments have to be intercepted and it is up to you to remain vigilant against these… eeeerrrgh, eeerrgmn [here Watts wrings his hands like a befuddled, *Annie Hall* era Woody Allen, pauses, and shrugs]. I now defer the remainder of my time to Senator Dethathuhagagh . . . [Watts walks from the stage, his robe trailing, to reveal a dancer who'd been hiding under it the whole time, who now performs a routine for the crowd].

We begin with a warning—foreboding, yes, but from an ally, who seeks to shake us from our complacency. But then the phrase "I know many of you" doesn't resolve the way we think it will—into something like "refuse to acknowledge the threat, and wish to remain with your loved ones." Instead, it becomes a parsing out of how close we and the speaker may be in our social networks—pedantic, picayune, and far from the ominous scene we've been in. Ashbery warps syntactic and tonal expectations in exactly the same way in his more adventurous long poems. In the passage that follows, about the distance between the truth and the centers of Andromeda, the better literary parallel is probably Milton, and those passages of *Paradise Lost* that depict infernal and cosmic space in terms that we simply can't assimilate to our terrestrial understanding. The juxtaposition of this with the speaker's sudden inability to know what to call those things against which we must remain vigilant is jarring: is this truly an authoritative speaker? And the sudden turn to the language of civic bureaucracy is no easier to assimilate than is the sudden, arbitrary appearance of the dancer from beneath Watts' character's robes.

•

How to make sense of Reggie Watts? Clearly he wants us to ask that question, and making us ask it is an important part of the act. But we still wonder—how did he come to be such an unusual performer? We usually turn to biography to answer questions like this, and Watts is happy to play with that genre. Google "Reggie Watts interview" sometime, and you'll find several fake interviews in which he 'reveals' nonsensical biographical information as an incomprehensible key to his aesthetic. Me, I like the one about the YMCA gym instructor and the shampoo.

•

There is one interview in which Watts conforms to the conventions and tells us about his background, which is, in fact, revealing. In contrast to Karl Pilkington, who is very much the product of a single, established community, Watts is something of an exotic—no matter what context you put him in. His mother was French, his father African-American, and he spent his childhood in Germany and Spain before settling in Great Falls, Montana, where he was one of very few people who weren't white. He found that people's only way to understand him came from representations of African-Americans on television and in the movies—a fact that made the artificiality and inaccuracy of those interpretive frameworks plain to him.

Not fitting into any group in high school, Watts decided to enter into the spirit of many groups, getting involved with the band geeks, and joining the football team—not to become a jock, but in order to see what the world of football was like. He continued this kind of behavior after completing school: he spent the 1990s playing in a huge number of bands in and around Seattle. To this day he is convincing as a musician in almost any genre: reggae, rap, heavy metal, classical, jazz. His background has never allowed him to simply be one thing, but it has allowed him to be many things, and, like his acts, to shift around among them. No lion, he, no Pilkington. Reggie Watts (I can almost hear him chuckling at the solemnity of this) is the wind.

·

AS DIFFERENT AS Watts is from Pilkington, we can still make sense of him with reference to Henri Bergson's theory of comedy as rigidity. Of course Watts' act isn't rigid at all—it's Heraclitan fluidity all the way through. But that's the point, really, at which it intersects with Bergson: Watts shows us the rigidity of any genre, of any mode of speech, and of any set of conventions—even of any identity. And this is a challenge to us. We need to be flexible to keep up. Watts has said his act is a kind of disruption, a matter of recontextualizing. "I look at things this way," said one interviewer, Reihan Salam, as he tried to summarize Watts' position. "I look at things this way, or the way my community looks at them… and suddenly I see Reggie Watts."

Watts agrees, and tells us that what he values is a kind of openness. "To be flexible, to be able to move freely . . . that's the thing I have to protect" Watts says. It matters, too, adds Watts, because it's essential to what human beings are—"they're explorers."

·

WHEN *THE WIND and the Lion* came out in 1975, it spoke to a post-Vietnam America that was rethinking its role as a global imperial power. Did our global role do some damage to our souls, depriving us of a sense of our identity? Ought we not to step back from local cultures—those noble lions—and let them roar? But everything looks different four decades later. Now, we're in a time of worldwide backlash against globalization, cosmopolitanism, and internationalism. Everywhere the lions roar—in a hyper-nationalist Russia, in a strong China that feels restricted by global institutions it didn't make, in a radicalized Middle East, and in the post-industrial rustbelt of an America that blames immigrants and international commerce for its woes. Eliot found Blake terrifying for seeing things only from his own particular perspective, for refusing to try to see from viewpoints alien to his own. Is Karl Pilkington terrifying? No one who looks at the soft, slightly confused eyes peering out from his bald, round head would think so. And I'm sure he's entirely humane. After all, despite his resistance to the wonders and cultures he encounters in his travels, he means, and does, no harm. But not all lions are tame and friendly, and we don't know how long, how strong, or in what direction, the wind will blow.

It's dark out there, people. We could all use a laugh.

MEAGAN CIESLA

Darlin' Sue

WE DON'T GET MANY EARTHQUAKES in Toledo. We don't get many tremors, either. We don't get many natural disasters at all, so a few weeks ago when I noticed the saltshaker shivering on the table, I headed straight for the doorway, sat in a ball on the floor, and started rocking back and forth. Gary came home after I'd already curled myself into the fetal position waiting for the house to come tumbling down around me. He saw me but instead of reaching out a hand to help me up he started laughing his head off. He said he hadn't felt anything on his drive home and that I was blowing things out of proportion. There I was weeping like a child, wearing my work scrubs, pressing myself into the filthy linoleum floor, and all he did was look at me like I was a joke and pat his stomach to signal he was going into the other room to root through the refrigerator. I told him he could blow himself out of proportion for all I cared, and slammed the door to the bedroom.

Since then, I'd been restless, irritated, and everything Gary did started to rub me the wrong way—how he ironed his jeans; how he ate the core of his apple; how he wiped each foot exactly three times on the welcome mat before coming inside.

"They're clean, Gary!" I'd yell to him. "All you did was walk to the mailbox and back, for Christ's sake!"

But he would just shrug his shoulders and say, "It's old habit."

Gary had been my first and only boyfriend. It's not that I'm ugly or anything, cause I'm not. I'm not saying I'm a super model, but I'm ok looking—I have two perfect mouthfuls of breast and my face is more or less symmetrical. But for one reason or another, things just never worked out between me and other men. Gary'd gone to four-year college and I knew he'd been with other girls before. When we met I was twenty-four and he knew he was my first; I think he found some kind of insurance policy in that. Deep down, I think he liked knowing he was the only guy I'd been with.

Gary works on paper clip patents for Hammermill. He makes sure each patent is up-to-date and that no one else in the office supply world has gotten hold of the company's design.

In all honesty, Gary's boringness is part of the reason we got married; I knew he'd never go anywhere and he knew I was a sure thing. I'd lived my whole adult life thinking there must be something wrong with me because there's got to be something wrong with a woman who lives almost a quarter of a century without having a single boyfriend. And I thought maybe he was the only one who hadn't noticed my defect, and if that was so, I should probably hold onto him. He was one of those guys that'd followed the straight and narrow: he knew how to do his own laundry, had a job and a mortgage on a house. I thought that's all I'd ever want.

How things change.

•

I CAUGHT MY new neighbor's dog digging up the tulips in our yard and was thrilled because it meant I would have to take him next door. I walked over to him and took him by his collar, then started pulling him back home. The dog was part Great Dane and part mongrel, a bastard dog, no doubt.

"Nina!" I called out, as I dragged the mutt behind me while he snotted on my hand then licked it off. "Niiiina!"

"Nina," I said once more, but by the time I finished calling her name she was out on her porch wondering what all the commotion was about. She was in black pedal pushers and a turquoise tank top that emphasized her firm breasts. She taught spinning and Pilates and her shoulders crested to catch the sunlight.

I dragged the Dane the rest of the way up the steps and Nina opened the door to let him back inside.

"Oh God, Sue, I'm so sorry. I don't know why he keeps jumping that fence."

"It's ok," I told her.

"What is this, the second time this week?"

"It's alright," I said. It was the third.

She looked back through the screen door and eyed the dog who'd found a place for himself in the hallway.

"I just don't know why he keeps doing that," she said.

She stood there with her smooth skin and collarbone catching sunlight, and I watched her run her fingers through her dark hair in a swift, adept stroke. Her hair was cropped short but not like a man's. It was more styled than that—the line of the cut framed her high-cheeked face.

Truth is, I may have had something to do with why the dog kept coming into my yard.

A while ago I saw a smashed squirrel on the side of the street so I put it in a baggy and buried it in the corner of our flowerbeds. The dog would get a whiff from the other side of the chain link fence and he couldn't resist. He'd dig it up and I'd rebury it after I took him back to Nina's house.

"You know dogs," I said. "They want to get out and see the world."

She told me she'd been on the phone with her sister in Norway and hadn't been paying attention to the dog out back.

"Norway," I said, trying to keep the conversation going. "Vikings!"

A long pause leaked between us and I could feel her losing interest, which made me heavy. I hoped it wasn't something I'd said. Up until then, I thought things had been going so well. I'd never talked to Nina for more than a few minutes, and I knew that if we clicked just one time, she'd invite me in. We'd make a tradition of it, me bringing over the dog, her inviting me in, making coffee. We'd talk about dentists and Pilates and hair removal.

"Well," I said after a long enough silence, "Guess I should get going."

"Thanks for returning Bo," she said.

"Who?" I asked, before remembering that Bo was the Dane's name. "Oh, sure. No problem. Anytime."

I started back home and when I heard her screen door shut I slowed my pace, hoping she would watch me make my way across her window.

Since she'd moved in, Nina'd been on my mind. I could see directly into her bedroom and living room from our house, so I knew a thing or two about her. First off, she had a lot of boyfriends. Sometimes I'd see them at night when Gary was sleeping. The men were always different and never stayed over. I wanted to ask her out right what her secret was, but didn't know how. The thought had crossed my mind that maybe she was charging them some kind of money, it must be hard living off of spinning and Pilates, but I didn't want to think that about her so I just assumed she really liked having sex. I was waiting until we became best friends to bring it up.

Second, she hardly had any furniture and most of her boxes remained unpacked in the living room. I liked that she was too busy to decide where her books should live. I wished I could be so carefree, but I had responsibilities and another person that tied me down.

When I got back to our yard from Nina's I found Gary hanging his tighty whities over the clothesline.

"What the hell are you doing?" I said, snatching the wet underwear off the line and throwing them back into the basket.

"You told me to do the laundry."

"Not out here, not like this. Everyone can see right in the yard."

"So?"

"So I don't want your unmentionables out here flapping in the wind!"

I was still bitter about him leaving me crouched in the doorway, as if that wasn't embarrassment enough. As if it would have been so hard for him to reach out a hand and help me up. Acknowledge how scary it must have been for me—the whole world caving in like that.

"Who cares," he said.

"I don't want the neighbors talking about it and I don't want them talking about me."

"They're *my* underwear."

"Good God, Gary. You just don't get it, do you?"

As I took the rest of the laundry down from the line, he walked away, moping, saying, "I don't know what's with you these days, Sue. That's what I don't get."

I could see Nina stirring something on the stove and I considered going back over and apologizing about the noise of our bickering and the soggy underwear, explaining that Gary didn't know much about couth. I thought if I went over to her now, there was still time to fix any bad impressions she had about me. Just then she looked out the window and gave me a little wave. I think she wanted me to know that things were still OK, that whatever Gary did with his wet laundry didn't hurt whatever was going on between us.

•

You know what I thought about in those five seconds under the doorway? I thought about how I'd been letting my life slip by. How I'd only ever slept with Gary and how, because of that, I'd been feeling sorry for myself for years and years. I was stuck on that thought for weeks until I decided that no one was going to dig me out of this hole except myself. I looked in the mirror after I got out of the shower and said: *Hey, Sadsack! Buck up! You've still got two perfect mouthfuls of breast on you!* And that made me feel better—knowing that there was still something ahead of me—that all hope wasn't lost.

When I decided to make my way out of feeling sorry for myself I figured the first thing I needed to do was to work on me. I got two cans of soup from the kitchen and started doing lunges every day. I'd walk across the room ten times before getting in the shower and going to work. Before I started, I would imagine people throwing quarters at my thighs and watch them bounce off like balls on a trampoline. All that positive thinking and knowing once I got some things together, I could really stand up for myself and leave Gary behind, must've been doing some good because the other dental hygienist at work, Trisha, told me I had a new glow about me.

I don't know about any glow, but the lunges with the soup cans had made me feel better. I got up the nerve to show up at Nina's door without the dog but with a jar of honey in hand instead.

Once I rang her doorbell and heard her coming down the steps I checked to see if I'd put on deodorant.

"Sue," she said. "Did Bo get out again?"

"No," I told her. "Nothing like that. Just honey."

I could tell she was confused so I held out the jar I brought with me.

"How sweet of you," she said, and opened the door for me. She showed me to the kitchen and put on tea. We talked and talked and we propped our feet up on the unpacked boxes scattered around the kitchen. Nina showed me the cowhide rug in her living room. I demonstrated the lunges I'd been doing and she gave me some pointers, made sure my knee wasn't sliding over my ankle. When we sat back down at the table I decided we were friends enough now to talk about our darkest secrets.

"You know Gary," I said, "My husband."

Nina nodded.

"Well, I've been thinking of cutting out on him."

"Like leaving?" Nina's perfectly arched eyebrows raised up at me and I followed the peak of her brow line. She was beautiful. "Why?" she asked.

"You know," I said to her.

"I do?"

"Sure. You're not married, right?"

Nina shook her head and laughed at the idea. "Me? I like married men," she said, "But I don't want to marry them."

"See. I knew you'd get it," I said. "You could have mine."

"Really," she said.

"Sure. Take him off my hands, see if I care."

Nina raised her eyebrows and the corners of her mouth lit up.

I told her about the tremors and the paper clips and how Gary'd wasted my youth.

She leaned into the table and patted my hand. She was following every one of my words and I was relieved to finally have someone's attention.

"Oh, Sue," she said. "I can't imagine what it must be like. You know, I almost got married once."

"You did?"

She nodded.

"What happened?"

"Well, I live a certain kind of lifestyle. And I just realized if I wanted to get married, I wouldn't be able to live the life I'd been living."

I told her that's *exactly* how I felt. Like Gary was holding me back from being the person I was supposed to be.

Gary was home making a chicken potpie. It was my favorite and he knew it and I thought maybe the potpie was his way of apologizing for not helping me up the day of the earthquake, or for holding me captive in the prime of my life when I was supposed to be out in the world sowing my oats, or for his wet underwear on the clothesline and his feet wiping ruining my life.

I asked him what the occasion was and he said, "Just thought you could use a nice meal."

That was sweet of him. He always had been a thoughtful man. Ever since we were first dating he made me lunch each day to take to work. It was always peanut butter with some flavor of jelly and it was smashed by the time I ate it, but at first I was so bowled over by the fact that I had a boyfriend and that he'd done something for me that I didn't much care.

We ate the potpie straight from the casserole dish while watching *Dateline* on the couch. When we were done eating Gary started inching his hand slowly up the thigh of my scrub pants, trying to get his fingers under the drawstring waistband. I only let it go on for two seconds cause I thought maybe I could just close my eyes and pretend it was someone else like I often did, but I couldn't go through with it.

Instead I turned to face him and said, "What in the hell are you doing?"

I wouldn't have been so harsh except he was still in his work clothes and I could hear a soft rattle in his shirt pocket as he moved his arm—undoubtedly loose paper-clips rustling around in the corners.

"What's it look like?"

"Well knock it off," I said, and brushed his hand away. "You have potpie breath."

Gary pushed himself off the couch, grabbed two Diet Cokes from the refrigerator, hollered, "You're driving me crazy, Sue! What do you want from me?" and went sulking out into the garage.

When I heard a crash a while later I looked out the window to find Gary, shirtless, kicking over trashcans into the alley. He was talking to himself in the backyard by the fence and waving his hands around. I hated myself for getting angry at him like that after he'd made potpie, but I just couldn't handle him anymore. I wanted to go over and talk to Nina about it, woman to woman, but there was no way to get there without running into Gary, and I thought he needed to cool off awhile. So I went upstairs into the bedroom and looked across the way.

Nina's bedroom light was on and she was in the middle of having sex with a man wearing nothing but a pair of leather chaps and a necktie; the guy was older than she was, balding but muscular, and she was holding onto his tie like she'd just lassoed him. I turned out my bedroom light and brought up a chair to the window to watch. It wasn't my first time watching Nina have sex. It happened fairly often, and I couldn't get over how much she seemed to love it. Whenever Gary and I had sex, I usually just waited it out and hoped his wounded squirrel grunts wouldn't last too long until he climbed off and started snoring into sleep. Sex seemed a sticky hassle to me and I'd always thought it was my problem—like maybe I wasn't a sexual being or something. Maybe I'd waited too long to lose my virginity and I'd lost my window of opportunity.

Nina slid the knot of the guy's tie closer to his neck and he started bucking. I grabbed my own throat, wondered what it must feel like to be reigned in, and then I stuck my hand down my underpants.

I hadn't counted on Gary coming into the bedroom.

I was so caught up in imagining how it must feel to be that man on Nina's bed, to be able to touch the soft the skin on the backs of her knees, that I hadn't heard

Gary's feet tromping up the steps. I didn't even notice him standing right behind me taking it all in.

"Thought you'd be in bed," he said, and I just about jumped out of my skin. I was so angry at him for creeping up behind me that I didn't say anything back. I crawled into bed and turned over onto my side.

Gary closed the curtains and brushed his teeth.

"That what you want?" he asked me just as I was crossing over the line into sleep.

I opened my eyes in the dark and could still see a sliver of Nina's window lit across the way. I thought to myself that that's what everyone wanted.

"So what if it is," I said to Gary, and then started breathing slow and heavy like I'd drifted off to sleep.

"Alright then," he said. "As long as you're sure."

•

I CAME HOME after assisting a root canal at work and found Gary on the couch wearing a neckerchief.

"Cold?" I asked as I stripped off the cardigan I wore to work.

It should have been obvious that I was making fun of him because it must have been at least 85 degrees that day and we only had one ceiling fan.

Gary took a long breath in before pulling on his Diet Coke, and then, only after I saw the lump of his Adam's apple rise and fall with a swallow, did he answer.

"Nope," he said, so matter-of-factly I had to second-guess myself about that rust colored paisley fabric tied around his throat.

"What's with the scarf?" I asked, but he just ignored me and crossed both of his feet atop the coffee table.

Then I found the planter that usually held my Christmas cactus empty for all but a layer of brown sludge lining the bottom. When I asked Gary if he knew what'd happened to my cactus he told me he'd needed something to spit in. He said it and I looked over to see a wad of chaw tucked inside his lip and a small brown thread lodged between his canine and his incisor, sitting there like a wedged in poppy seed. Gary'd never shown any interest in tobacco. In fact, he'd made a point of it to scowl at smokers we passed outside of bars and restaurants as if to say to them: you're killing everyone around you too, pal.

"What the hell's the gunk in your teeth, Gar?"

He took his thumbnail to the middle of his front teeth. "That it?"

I told him yes even though I could still see it sitting right where it had been before.

"When'd you start chewing tobacco?" I asked as I unlaced my shoes and put them by the door.

"Can't recall," he said as he dug in the front pocket of his shirt, got out a can of Copenhagen, and stuffed a new gob in his lip.

"Well I think it's disgusting," I said.

Gary swiped the planter from my hands and shot a big wad out the side of his mouth but his aim was way off and the sludge landed right on the big toe of my bare foot. I looked at Gary but he didn't even seem sorry. He just tucked the planter under his arm and headed out into the garage.

I didn't know what to make of the chaw chewing Gary. I thought he was probably just trying to get back at me for not giving him sex the other day. He probably expected me to apologize for the comment about his potpie breath, but I wasn't falling for it. Plus, at least it wasn't the old Gary. This Gary didn't even bother to wipe his shoes on the mat—he just tromped on in bringing everything from the outside world into our living room on the soles of his feet.

Somebody must've figured out about the dead squirrel cause Bo hadn't been in the yard for several days and when I went out to see if it was still there all I found were small holes in between the tulips. I went over to Nina's house with a loaf of banana bread as an excuse to visit but she didn't answer even though her car was in the garage and I could see her through her living room curtains. I thought maybe Nina had finally figured out what everybody else but Gary had known—that there was something wrong about me. And if only she would let me know what it was I needed to fix, I would do it. I knew I could change.

Gary and I hardly talked anymore. I'd come home from work to find him on the couch practicing rope ties and chewing tobacco. He started wearing jeans to work and stopped calling me by name. He'd been saying it for more than a decade but it was like he just woke up one day and couldn't say it anymore. When he did talk to me he called me Darlin'. He didn't even try to say Sue. It was just Darlin' this and Darlin' that.

•

I WAS SCRUBBING bean scum from a pot Gary had cooked with the night before when I spotted him on the ground in our yard with his arm looped around Bo's neck. At first, I thought Gary'd caught the Dane in the tulips again—maybe the squirrel had been there all along—but then I realized that wasn't the case at all. Gary was doing everything he could to get that dog on its back. Bo was yelping and scurrying its legs to keep balance, but Gary finally managed to flip him and as soon as the dog's shoulders hit the grass, Gary let him go and the dog went shooting around the yard.

"Gar," I yelled to him out the back door. "What're you doing?"

"I was bulldogging that damn dog," he said.

"Why'd you do that?" I asked him.

By the time I got myself outside, I noticed Nina was sitting in a lawn chair wearing a sunhat, cheering Gary on.

"He got 5.5," she said.

"Is that good?"

"Could be better for a Dane," Nina said. "Could be worse."

Even though I'd been over to Nina's a dozen times, she'd never stepped foot on our property before.

Gary went over to the fence and leaned one arm against it, right beside her chair.

"How long've you been out here?" I asked Nina.

"Who knows," she said as she crossed her legs. The skin of her calves glistened from the lotion that must've been on them. "A while, I guess."

"Maybe you should get inside. That sun'll burn you right through today."

"I'm fine," she told me. "I've got on 45."

"Those numbers don't mean anything, really," I said.

"Why don't you go back inside and put some coffee on, Darlin?" Gary said. "Nina and I are catching up."

Catching up? I thought to myself. You only catch up with old friends, not strangers. And everyone knows that Nina's my friend and not Gary's.

"Nina," I said, ignoring Gary. "Maybe we can get together later this afternoon and go over those crunches you were showing me?"

Nina took a sip from her iced coffee and said, "Maybe another day would be better," then went back to scratching Bo under his chin and giving Gary pointers about leveraging his leg under the dog's hips for a smoother flip.

I didn't like that Nina was giving Gary tips on how to beat out her own dog; that didn't seem like the loyal thing to do. And then she started laughing at something Gary said and it made me wonder if maybe Gary was funnier than I realized he was, and *then* I thought that *I* should be the one being funny, not him. But I hadn't been funny, not for a long time. Maybe ever.

•

GARY STOPPED ASKING me what was wrong all the time and never made me lunch anymore, not even peanut butter and jelly sandwiches that ended up smashed by the time I went to eat them, but I started making his. Half the time I'd find them thrown the trashcan in the alley still in the bag. I barely even saw him except at dinner when we ate in front of the TV. He started going out at night and leaving me home all alone. He said he needed some space. If you ask me, it wasn't fair for him to ask for space.

I was the one who needed space. I was the one who was thinking about leaving *him*. I was the one with the space problem.

I spent a lot of time waiting up for Gary. I thought about how you thought you knew the person you married until something like this happened, and it turned out you didn't know them at all. I would get those cheap romance novels at the grocery store and try and make myself fall asleep, but I couldn't keep my mind from racing. Before, I used to spend my nights awake thinking of what I would say to him when I left. How I would only walk out with one bag on my shoulder and leave the rest behind. But after I started to wait up I just spent those long quiet hours wishing him back home. When I asked him in the mornings where he'd been the night before, he just said, "Out," and that was the end of that. I never had any real reason not to believe him. I mean, this was Gary we're talking about. The paperclip guy. There's no reason I shouldn't rest safe and sound knowing that he was the same man who promised me for better or worse.

As I was finishing up my latest romance one night I noticed Nina's bedroom light come on. I hadn't talked to her in a while and I hadn't seen her with anyone else, either. I knew she'd had men in there but she'd started leaving her bedroom light off. Maybe all those afternoons we'd spent in her kitchen didn't mean anything after all.

I pulled the chair up to the window and grabbed my glasses so I could see better. Nina was on top, all aglow, her hands running through her hair. She was beautiful like that, balancing on top. Her breasts were bouncing up and down and to see her happy made me calm again. Maybe there was still hope for us; maybe she just needed time.

Nina put her hands down on the bed and flipped over so she was the one pinned onto the sheets. The man's back was just muscular enough that I could make out shadows beneath the shoulder blades; his back was strong but not threatening, and I could see how Nina would like that about him. The back of his neck was long and pale and there was something about it I recognized but couldn't place it until he turned around and stared at me through the window. His face was one I'd seen every day for ten years but it didn't register because nothing I knew about Gary could let him be the man on top of Nina, naked all the way down except a pair of chaps. When he saw me he gave a smile across the way, as if he was happy to see me—as if he hadn't seen me in some time. Once he waved it sank in that it must be Gary, my husband, *my* Gary, over there. I rushed over and started banging the hell out of Nina's door. Bo was jumping up and barking his head off at me, but I didn't care, I was miles beyond fear. When Nina finally got to the door in a robe half covering her, she barely had time to open it before I bulldogged her onto the hardwood, pantyless and all. I put her in a headlock and could feel her long, delicate soft neck in the crook of my arm. She was sweaty and her nipples were hard; she tried to scream my name but her words were barely recognizable with all the air I was squeezing out of her windpipe.

Whatever Nina and I had had was over. I knew that as soon as Gary looked over across the way and smiled at me. She wasn't the woman I thought she was and I could see that now. I looked right into her eyes as she was staring up at me begging for air. She was flapping like a fish and her legs were splayed wide open wafting the smell of trout guts in my face. I looked right at her crotch and saw Gary's condom hanging limp between her legs, still halfway inside of her. It was like she was trying to rub it in, her and Gary, even though I was on top pinning her to the hardwood. She wasn't at all the person I knew.

Gary never did come downstairs. He hovered at the top of the staircase with an erection that wouldn't quit, a pair of chaps on, his hands on his hips looking triumphant. He looked good up there like that, like a bull rider who'd just ridden his first eight seconds, but I couldn't handle seeing him look that proud after what he'd done.

There was nothing to say except, "Put your dick away, Gary. For Christ sakes! You're my Goddamned husband. Doesn't that mean anything to you? Jesus Christ."

Gary tried to tuck his erection into the waist of his chaps but it wouldn't go. He looked down and me and at Nina and all he said was, "You gave it the OK, Sue. You gave it the OK."

•

I KICKED GARY out, but he wouldn't go far. I told him I didn't mean what I said about Nina having him, that it was a joke. But he said it didn't sound like I was joking, so how was he to know? He said he'd promised he'd never leave me, so he kept his word. He built a tent out of tarps that night and he'd been sleeping in it ever since. Each morning I check to see if he was still there, and he always was.

It's not that I didn't want to invite him in. Nina went away to visit her sister in Norway and I wanted to pretend none of it had ever happened—that I hadn't thought about leaving him, that Nina'd never moved next door, that I hadn't been so nasty to Gary in the first place or hadn't fallen for Nina. But I couldn't take it back. Not now.

I gave up on my soup can squats. I replaced them with breakfast at the Cinnabon in the mall. That and a large skim mocha with whipped cream because I needed something to look forward to so I would get out of bed.

Between patients I'd try and see how much Novocain it would take to numb my nose just so I would have something to concentrate on. I'd shoot two shots usually, maybe three, then pinch it in front of the mirror until I couldn't feel a thing. It was nice having something that I could still control. I knew that no matter what, if I put that Novocain in my nose, it would numb. Seems like my nose was the only thing that could get numb—every other part of me felt broken down.

When the Novocain wasn't enough, I tried other things to make me feel better. There was a tooth extraction scheduled one afternoon and I'd just put the patient down. He wasn't terrible looking; he was a Verizon Wireless salesman who'd been coming in for a couple of years and I felt like we knew each other well enough. He'd sold me my cell phone a few months ago and had given me a good deal on a data plan. He still had most of his hair and swore he flossed twice a day, though I had my doubts. Right after he was under I leaned in and kissed him, just to see what it would be like. I wanted to make myself move on already. I stayed there with my lips against his for a while, hoping something would happen. That all the hurt I'd been feeling about Gary and Nina would dissolve. But I didn't feel a thing except his chapped lips and cotton mouth, and then Trisha started banging on the door with her giant arm asking if I was alright so I had to make like I was prepping the room before she opened the door and caught me.

Once I *did* let Gary come in for spaghetti dinner, but I couldn't look at him without being sick to my stomach. Knowing he had wanted Nina, even if for a minute, was too much. You can't just make things go back to being ok again; it's not that easy.

•

I LEAVE FOR the office each morning and pass him on the way out, shoo him away like a stray and tell him to get. But he doesn't budge. He just tends to his pit fire and pees on the tulips. He says he'll be there in the evening when I come home from work, that he'll wait for me to get over it. I beg him to go away and leave me be, but he keeps saying that time will make things better; it always does. He says we made up our minds a while ago, for better or for worse.

This morning I looked outside and saw Gary cooking biscuits over his pit fire. He's never really apologized, he said he was just trying to make me happy—all he wanted was to be able to give me what I needed to make me happy and isn't that what marriage is all about? I never know how to answer that, but I think about it every night while listening to him in the backyard, playing his harmonica by his little campfire.

JUNED SUBHAN

The Swan I

A swan's scream through a funnel of sky,

and my father scooping quilts of snow
with a rusty shovel
until his lungs collapsed as he stared ahead:
my mother beside a grave of swans
near the frozen, blue lake.

Only last winter, I
remembered the swans huddled together
across the lake like a choir of beautiful, young women
dressed in shimmering sheath-gowns.

My mother retrieved one of the swans,
half-breathing,
half-alive,
its slender neck in a twist.

Sometimes, the swans flew over

our home, and when my mother
caught sight of them,

she said if she got hold of one,
she'd use its wings and feathers
to sew frilly, winter dresses for me and herself,

or a cloak for my father.

He lay in bed,

in the attic,
naked, sexless,

sniffling with an oxygen mask strapped
over his lilac mouth,
dreaming of shovelling more snow,
eyes glazed with the wreckage of winter,
his cool-pink lungs visible through his transparent chest.
He struggled to breathe, and I thought soon

my father's skin would turn as white as the swan
my mother brought into the house,

suckling it at the kitchen table.

"It will be nursed back to its former self," she said,
even though I noticed a vein of blood and breast milk
on the swan's beak,

staining its feathers.

Still, I heard

my father sniffle in my ears, my mother rocking

back and forth in the red oak rocking chair,
cradling the dying swan.

I believe there must be
several other graves outside,
graves that had recently been dug out,

filled with hundreds and hundreds of swans,

and my father in my mother's arms,
caught in a funnel of sky, and

falling.

The Swan II

My mother said she'd witnessed a choir of swans
plummeting down from the curved glass of the sky,

like comets of flaming-white fire,
white fire growing brighter and brighter

as they spiralled down with greater speed.
She continued to nurse the half-dead swan,

feeding it her own milk, milk squeezed
into a tube and so white, I believe she must have

crushed into powder a set of baby's teeth or bones
to produce a milk so white. She coffined the swan in

tufts of cream satin and laid it on the kitchen table,
next to a bowl of sliced, blood oranges, its neck still in a twist—

sweet Jesus crucified, my sweet love, my sweet, empty home,
wrapped in a spine of light and feathers on a gold cross.

Her laughter travelled all the way up to the attic,
where my father lay, her voice making a low, flute sound.

He did not whisper a word,
and I realize his lungs will one day become

so diaphanous they'll no longer exist.
As he breathed in, the inside

of his oxygen mask became lined with prickles of silver,
as though the oxygen canister was filled with dry ice.

I glanced out of the attic window, towards
somewhere distant where love had been lost,

my gaze catching a spray of white wings,
in winter's white haze. I recalled

when my father had been shovelling a heap of snow
during the previous winter,

my mother squeezed my shoulder,
then uttered in my ear,

Look baby, the swans have gathered by the lake,
swans falling from a low sky. She hadn't noticed my father fall.

The Swan III

It died first thing this morning, my mother said
in the kitchen, the dead swan
lying in a twist on the table.

She then gathered the swan in her arms; its slender
neck hung over her elbow like a wreathe of flame-white hair
and she said, *I'll be home soon, tell your father I loved him.*

Through the window, I saw her disappear
further into deeper snow, while
beyond her faint outline, the swans finally

rose from their grave, not just one but
hundreds and hundreds of them,
shrieks and wings in an open field of air,

hundreds and hundreds of swans carrying
the ghosts of feathers with them,
and my mother singing one final hymn.

Once she reached the grave, she found it empty,
gazing into a hollow ditch, and the swan
in her arms slid down over the curve of her embrace.

Glancing back, she no longer saw her own home,
and the whistle of my father's lungs,
sinking and rising filled the house.

His oxygen mask swirled with whispers of snow
until he ceased to breathe. I gazed out of the window,
my empty room, my empty home, seeing

for the very first time, the bright living world:
a grave, my father shoveling snow and
my mother murdering swans.

CHELSEA DINGMAN

Fetal Monitor

My mother didn't understand why I had children
so late.   Years of complaining to my husband
that marriage is only paper
          & what happens to paper
                              when it gets wet? She wanted
a baby to hold before
she was too old to remember
          her teeth. At the funeral, a box so small
it could be for a cat.   She asks why
did this happen, what do the doctors say,
          will this happen again?   But what does it matter
why?
          Who can think   about what a good risk
love is, in a place we're not safe
          from ourselves?
          Pray, she says. Pray
                    the next one   has a stronger heart. But
who would welcome another   child to dust
their mantel?   I think back to swelling before
          the bathroom mirror, each month
twisting inside me.   I tracked our progress
in photographs,
          waiting to reclaim myself. I wanted her
but I wanted myself more, some days. That's the truth.
I want to feel her move
          inside me now. To let her feed
from my blood   & know my body
isn't a holding cell
          for ghosts.   I'm grateful
my mother doesn't say she's sorry
          for my loss. There's no good answer
when people say that.   I held her in the hospital long enough
to trace her mouth
          & beg   for sound.

Visibility

Somewhere, someone knows who I am. My mother,
dead. My father, lost to train stations & ports of call. When the social

insurance office asks me for a list of dependents,
I have no box to check. The man who killed my daughter, dragged

before a judge, pleaded guilty. I'm inspected for house code
violations after my wife & sons die, while the creek thrashes

over rocks in the back yard. I answer no questions for anyone.
I know how to play this game, the cell they'll throw me in

if I swerve from the one lane of dirt road leading home
from a bar. I'll pretend that this is what happens to someone

born into war, a field of broken bodies, the birds unfeathered
in a stiff wind. I'll pretend I've learned how to move in a world

not at war. All of the places I've known shelter as a body
I bury myself in. The places I know shelter still.

JAMES DUNLAP

Night Fishing

I'm back to the oldest forms: time and darkness.
The boat knocking   in a crow-black lake, moon
like a bleached turtle shell,   fog nuzzling our hands
My father   fishes point, easing us   along the bank
under the gnarled backs of lake-trees, his spotlight flickering
waterline to tree-line   —spiders falling   from their wires of light
a cottonmouth   yawning on a branch,   its reeking mouth
dishinged   as if he was eating what's left of the night.
My father believes pain   is the best teacher: the rusty whistle
of the yo-yo   tripped too early,   he throws the oil-gummed pliers
to snap the hook shank from my fist, my hand, this crippled
fish bleeding   from its mouth. There is something blooming
and swelling   like a bed of catfish   in that quiet.
He has always said he's dead, his bones just haven't rotted yet.
So I imagine my father as an old church piano,   all rotten legs and splayed keys,
but here,   I only have a mind of water   and he is still rotten
rotten   like the cracked open mouth   of a dead gar—
each curved tooth   a shard of yanked starlight.

KYLE McCORD

On Size and Scope in The Arnolfini Portrait

After *The Arnolfini Portrait*, 1434

The pregnant woman's arms are heavy
       as stone cookware and ache powerfully

better to be the dog
       slavering over marrow

she thinks better a cobble a figment
       not the round observatory

of the unborn what but a woman
       must carry another world
          inside her body

without complaint though if it isn't nausea
          it's insomnia

at night she can see
       stars pushing through the swelling dark
       crowning crowning
       over the cathedral

damn their luck damn the painter's
       gaunt fingers the monstrous deer
       treading the hill like monks

who've stumbled onto holy ground
       such grace in their strides

once she cried
        for one doe's rumpled
        hide over its womb

the creature's panic so
        familiar
        she watched her testing the weight
        of half-rotten fruit
the deer glanced up

as if seeking blessing she struggled
        to remember a psalm
                as the deer panteth for the apple . . .

her husband scribbled away
        while the doe's eyes never left her
                as flesh and fruit
        dripped from its mouth

both of us filled she thought
        heavy with hunger's gravity

SARA ELIZA JOHNSON

Titan (I)[1]

Ligeia Mare

In the shadow lake
under the lake, in the zone
of your skeleton

a tremor flowers:
a cell blooms:
nucleoplasm spreading

like a moon submerged,
then a flash of acetylene,
its nuclear eye—

and soon you can breathe
in this liquid mirror—
and though not whole

your thought has found
a shape. When a deep
wave erupts beneath you,

through your plasma
like a voice in static, you float
from the bottom

of the shadow to its surface
where you release
your wound: the island

---

[1] These three "Titan" poems are written after the methane lakes of Titan, one of Saturn's moons.

that one day someone
will probe for life, try
to decipher. The lake

ripples against you
and, grateful to be touched,
you ripple back.

Titan (II)

Kraken Mare

As a storm forms above the lake, capillary waves open across it, and soon
a dark wind spirals the vapor into rain, and then rain and hail
      slit the waves
           into waves,

like the desert wind that had once slept beneath your corpse's eyelids
and had rippled them open,
          before the fire ants had eaten them,

as a wind had once disemboweled you, hollowed out your face so that light
      pooled into your skull,
          as water into a cave.

Now you open your new eyes in this lake—
              or not quite your eyes but a memory
of sight—as like blood vessels the waves open in you—

and the warmth settles back into you, as you remember the sun on your face
and how someone had laughed and taken your hands, and in some other
moment the weight of the sun and the blood vessel burst in your eye
      from crying

—you the brightest mote in the eye of the lake
              that opens for you, lets you
grow your mind deeper within it, and which through you learns the miracle
      of mitosis: a kind of breathing through dream.

Titan (III)

Jingpo Lacus

You step into the lake
and it holds you
as if it already knows
your form, has felt you before.
Like a wave circling back
your body steps
through itself.
       You step through the lake
and your skin opens
to let the ultraviolet in,
from which a crystal
seeds, and more crystals
grow, until your spine
is radiant reef
and your heart bleeding
out the species of darkness
that will populate
its glow.
       From above,
the lake is an iris,
with its pupil widening
to eclipse the blue:
your blood cells,
microscopic black stars
still proliferating below
its shining surface.
       You rise from the lake
like a cloud of oil,
a reflection climbing
from its mirror
or the pain from the wound
or the trauma
from an eye—break

between the break,
through which love arrives
to flood.

PATRICK ERRINGTON

Gleaning

On hands and knees, you take what you call
the middle ground. If a god can be found
here, it's because he couldn't commit either,

combing, like waves, the shingle, wanting
just some scrap worth settling on. Life,
at least, has settled on your body like silt

on that wreck no one else survived. When
you, daily, wake, it's as if washed ashore.
When you wish, it's a hundred liferafts'

beacons swimming in the dark. Imagine
a language where these are no different.
You pray and it's enough. Instead you lie

awake, knotting sheets, small hours heaped
up like driftwood. You could manage, make
do, get by, and you can. But there's a loss

for every light, for every sense's salvage.
Just to be alive to this world is an act of war.
You know to take a hand, some small thing

will go unheld. Hands alone keep loss
from reclamation. Only in this language
is the sky really less than heaven.

Bios

DILRUBA AHMED's poetry debut, *Dhaka Dust* (Graywolf, 2011), won the Bakeless Prize. Her poems have appeared in *American Poetry Review, Blackbird, New England Review,* and *Poetry.* The recipient of *The Florida Review* Editors' Award and a Dorothy Sargent Rosenberg Memorial Prize, she teaches at Bryn Mawr College.

JESSICA GUZMAN ALDERMAN's work has appeared or is forthcoming in *Meridian, The Normal School, Sonora Review,* and elsewhere. She is a PhD student at the University of Southern Mississippi's Center for Writers.

Poet and critic **ROBERT ARCHAMBEAU**'s most recent books are *Inventions of a Barbarous Age: Poetry from Conceptualism to Rhyme* (Madhat, 2016) and *The Kafka Sutra* (2015). He teaches at Lake Forest College.

MICHAEL BAZZETT's debut collection, *You Must Remember This* (Milkweed, 2014), received the Lindquist & Vennum Prize. His second collection, *Our Lands Are Not So Different,* was published by Horsethief Books in 2017, and he has two books forthcoming: a poetry collection titled *The Interrogation* and a verse translation of *The Popul Vuh,* the Mayan creation epic—both from Milkweed. He lives in Minneapolis with his wife and two children.

KATE BERSON is currently collaborating with Velma García-Gorena on a translation of Gabriela Mistral's *Poema de Chile.* While pursuing an MFA at UMass Amherst, Berson worked as a Delaney Fellow with Fiction Collective Two. Her fiction appears in *Denver Quarterly, Green Mountains Review, The Iowa Review, Western Humanities Review,* and elsewhere.

TALIA BLOCH has published poems in *The Antioch Review, Poetry International, Prairie Schooner, The Southern Review,* and elsewhere. She has received an Editors' Prize for Emerging Poets from *Pleiades* and her essays and feature stories have appeared in *The Brooklyn Rail, theForward,* and *TabletMagazine,* among others.

Originally from Flint, Michigan, **SARAH CARSON** is the author of two poetry collections: *Poems in Which You Die* (BatCat, 2014) and *Buick City* (Mayapple, 2015). Her work has appeared in *Columbia Poetry Review, Cream City Review, Nashville Review, New Orleans Review,* and elsewhere. She lives in Chicago.

ANDREW CARTWRIGHT studies in the MFA program at George Mason University, where he works for the journals *Phoebe* and *So To Speak*. His writing has appeared in *Esquire Ukraine* and *Word Riot*.

WENDY CHEN was awarded the Aliki Perrotti and Seth Frank Most Promising Young Poet Prize by the Academy of American Poets in 2014. Her poems have been published or are forthcoming in *American Poets*, *Cider Press Review*, *The McNeese Review*, and the anthology *Translations from World Literature*.

MEAGAN CIESLA's fiction and nonfiction have appeared in *Cimarron Review*, *The Collagist*, *Kenyon Review*, *The Long Story*, and other publications. She teaches at Gonzaga University in Spokane, Washington.

Originally from Chicago, **MARGARET CIPRIANO** is an MFA candidate at Ohio State University. Her visual and written work has appeared or is forthcoming in *Adroit Journal*, *DIAGRAM*, *Quarterly West*, *West Branch*, and elsewhere. She serves as managing editor of *The Journal*.

CHELSEA DINGMAN is a Canadian poet. Her first book, *Thaw*, won the National Poetry Series and is forthcoming in 2017 from the University of Georgia Press. In 2016, she won *The Southeast Review*'s Gearhart Poetry Prize, and her forthcoming work can be found in *Mid-American Review*, *Ninth Letter*, and *Third Coast*, among others.

VIET DINH is the author of *After Disasters* (Little A, 2016), which was a finalist for the PEN/Faulkner Award for Fiction, and his stories have appeared in *Chicago Review*, *Fence*, *Threepenny Review*, *Zoetrope: All-Story*, and elsewhere. The recipient of an NEA Fellowship and an O. Henry Prize, Dinh teaches at the University of Delaware.

JEHANNE DUBROW's sixth poetry collection, *Dots & Dashes*, won the Crab Orchard Review Series Open Competition Award and is forthcoming from SIU Press in 2017. Her previous collections include *The Arranged Marriage* (U. of New Mexico, 2015) and *Red Army Red* (Northwestern UP, 2012). She teaches at the University of North Texas.

JAMES DUNLAP's poems have appeared in *The Dirty Napkin*, *Heron Tree*, *Nashville Review*, *Weave*, and elsewhere. He lives in Arkansas.

PATRICK ERRINGTON is a poet and translator from Alberta, Canada. Winner of the 2016 London Magazine Poetry Prize, his poems have appeared in the 2016 *Best New Poets* anthology, *American Literary Review*, *The Iowa Review*, *West Branch*, and elsewhere. He is a doctoral candidate at the University of St. Andrews in Scotland.

Born in Tennessee and raised in Wisconsin, **GRAHAM FOUST** is the author of six books of poems, including *Time Down to Mind* (Flood, 2015) and *To Anacreon in Heaven and Other Poems* (2013). With Samuel Frederick, he has translated three books by the late German poet Ernst Meister, including *Wallless Space* (Wave, 2014). He teaches at the University of Denver.

JOHN GALLAHER's fifth and sixth poetry collections are *In a Landscape* (BOA, 2014) and *Ghost/Landscape* (BlazeVOX, 2016; with Kristina Marie Darling). He has edited two books—most recently Michael Benedikt's *Time Is a Toy* (U. of Akron, 2014)—and teaches at Northwest Missouri State University, where he edits *The Laurel Review*.

VELMA GARCÍA-GORENA teaches government and Latin American and Latino/a Studies at Smith College. Her translation of the complete correspondence between Gabriela Mistral and Doris Dana will be published by the University of New Mexico Press in 2018. She us currently translating Gabriela Mistral's political essays, working on a book manuscript on resistance to the border fence in the U.S. Southwest, and, with Kate Berson, she is translating Mistral's *Poema de Chile*.

TONY HOAGLAND's fifth poetry collection is *Application for Release from the Dream* (Graywolf, 2015). His second volume of critical essays is *Twenty Poems That Could Save America and Other Essays* (2014). He teaches at the University of Houston.

CYNTHIA HOGUE's ninth collection of poems is *In June the Labyrinth* (Red Hen, 2017). Her recent poems appear in *Best American Poetry 2016, Crazyhorse, Field, Kestrel,* and *Southern Indiana Review*. A 2015 NEA Fellow in Translation, Hogue teaches at Arizona State University.

SARA ELIZA JOHNSON is the author of *Bone Map* (Milkweed, 2014), which won the National Poetry Series. The recipient of an NEA Fellowship, a Rona Jaffee Foundation Writers' Award, and two Winter Fellowships from the Fine Arts Work Center in Provincetown, she teaches at the University of Alaska Fairbanks.

GENEVIEVE KAPLAN's debut collection is *In the ice house* (Red Hen, 2011), winner of the A Room of Her Own Foundation's poetry publication prize. Recent poems appear in *BOATT, Denver Quarterly*, and *Sugar House Review*. She lives in southern California.

ASHLEY KEYSER taught for several years in the Ukraine and currently lives in Chicago. Her work has appeared in *Best New Poets, The Cincinnati Review, Pleiades, Passages North,* and elsewhere.

KEITH KOPKA's poetry and criticism have recently appeared in *The International Journal of the Book*, *Mid-American Review*, *New Ohio Review*, *Ninth Letter*, and elsewhere. An assistant editor of *Narrative Magazine*, a recipient of a Chautauqua Arts Fellowship, and a Vermont Studio Center poetry fellow, he directs the creative writing program at Florida State University.

KIMBERLY KRUGE is a poet and translator based in Mexico. Her recent publications include poems (in either English or Spanish) in *The Glasgow Review of Books*, *Luvina*, *The Missouri Review*, *The Wisconsin Review*, and elsewhere.

PETER LaBERGE is the author of the chapbooks *Makeshift Cathedral* (YesYes, 2017) and *Hook* Sibling Rivalry, 2015). His recent work appears in *Best New Poets*, *Crazyhorse*, *Harvard Review*, *Iowa Review*, *Tin House* and elsewhere. A recent graduate of the University of Pennsylvania, LaBerge is founder and editor-in-chief of *The Adroit Journal* and has received a fellowship from the Bucknell Univeristy Stadler Center for Poetry.

JOSEPH O. LEGASPI, a Fulbright and New York Foundation for the Arts fellow, is the author of two poetry collections from CavanKerry Press: *Threshold* (2017) and *Imago* (2007). His work has appeared in *New England Review*, *Orion*, *Poetry*, the Academy of American Poets' Poem-a-Day, and elsewhere. He co-founded Kundiman, a non-profit organization serving Asian American literature, and lives in Queens, NY.

SHARA LESSLEY's forthcoming second collection is *The Explosive Expert's Wife*; her first collection is *Two-Headed Nightingale* (New Issues, 2012). Her awards include NEA and Stegner Fellowships, a Mary Wood Fellowship from Washington College, the Diane Middebrook Fellowship from the University of Wisconsin, and Colgate University's O'Connor Fellowship. The Operations Director for Oxford Writer's House in England, Lessley is currently editing an anthology of essays on poetry and place with the poet Bruce Snider.

LI QINGZHAO (1084-1151) is considered the greatest female poet in Chinese history, though only one English translation of her complete works is in print today. Her *ci*—poems set to songs with predetermined meters and tones—were gathered into the collection *Rinsing Over Jade*, which has since been lost to scholars. For more information, see page 19.

ADRIAN C. LOUIS grew up in northern Nevada and is an enrolled member of the Lovelock Paiute Tribe. From 1984-97, Louis taught at Oglala Lakota College on the Pine Ridge Reservation in South Dakota. He recently retired from teaching English at Southwest Minnesota State University. Pleiades Press published his latest book of poems, *Random Exorcisms*, in 2016.

KYLE McCORD is the author of six books of poetry, most recently *Magpies in the Valley of Oleanders* (Trio House, 2016). Recent work has been published in *Agni*, *Boston Review*, *Crazyhorse*, *Ploughshares*, and elsewhere. The recipient of grants from the Academy of American Poets, the Vermont Studio Center, and the Baltic Writing Residency, he edits Gold Wake Press and teaches at Drake University.

Work by **ALEX McELROY** appears in *The Atlantic*, *The Georgia Review*, *Kenyon Review Online*, *New England Review*, *Tin House*, and elsewhere. His chapbook, *Daddy Issues*, won the 2016 Editors' Prize from The Cupboard Pamphlet.

DAVID McLOGHLIN is an Irish poet and literary translator in the US since 2013. His first collection, *Waiting for Saint Brendan and Other Poems* (Salmon, 2012), won second prize in Ireland's Patrick Kavanagh Awards. His translation of Enrique Winter's *Sign Tongue* won the 2014 Goodmorning Menagerie Chapbook-in-Translation prize, and his second collection, *Santiago Sketches*, is forthcoming from Salmon in 2017.

POUPEH MISSAGHI is a writer and translator, and serves as Iran's editor-at-large for *Asymptote*. She has published translations from Persian in *Asymptote*, *Denver Quarterly*, *World Literature Today*, as well as several books into Persian in Iran. Her writing, fiction and nonfiction have appeared in *The Brooklyn Rail*, *Feminist Wire*, *Guernica*, *World Literature Today*, and elsewhere.

GABRIELA MISTRAL (born Lucila Godoy Alcayaga, 1889-1957) was a Chilean poet, educator, diplomat, and human rights activist who won the Nobel Prize in Literature in 1945. For more information, see page 69.

Recent fiction by **JOEL MORRIS** appears in *American Review*, *The Citron Review*, *Prick of the Spindle*, and elsewhere. He lives in Colorado.

JOANNA PEARSON's stories appear in *Blackbird*, *Carve*, *The Hopkins Review*, *New Madrid*, and elsewhere, and have been noted as distinguished in *Best American Short Stories 2015* and anthologized in *Best of the Net 2016*.

KEVIN PRUFER's forthcoming seventh poetry collection is *How He Loved Them* (Four Way, 2018); his sixth collection is *Churches* (Four Way, 2014). His recent co-editing projects include the forthcoming *Into English: An Anthology of Multiple Translations* (Graywolf, 2018) and *Literary Publishing in the Twenty-First Century* (Milkweed, 2016). He teaches at the University of Houston.

Poems by **STEPHANIE ROGERS** appear in *The Cincinnati Review*, *Pleiades*, *Ploughshares*, *The Southern Review*, and elsewhere. He first poetry collection, *Plucking the Stinger* (2016) was published by Saturnalia Books.

ELIZABETH SCANLON edits *The American Poetry Review* and is the author of the full-length collection *Lonesome Gnosis* (Horsethief, 2017). She has also published two chapbooks: *The Brain Is Not the United States/The Brain Is the Ocean* (The Head & The Hand, 2016), the title poem of which won a Pushcart, and *Odd Regard* (Ixnay, 2013).

HASANTHIKA SIRISENA's debut collection of stories *The Other One* (U of Massachusetts, 2016) won the Juniper Prize for fiction. Her work has appeared in *Epoch*, *Glimmer Train*, *The Globe and Mail*, *The Kenyon Review*, and elsewhere. She teaches at Susquehanna University.

ANALICIA SOTELO's forthcoming book of poems, *Virgin* (Milkweed, 2018), won the inaugural Jake Adam York Prize. Her poems appear in *The Antioch Review*, *The Boston Review*, *The New Yorker*, and elsewhere, and her chapbook, *Nonstop Godhead*, won the Poetry Society of America's 2016 Chapbook Fellowship. Sotelo is director of communications and development at Writers in the Schools in Houston.

PETE STEVENS edits fiction for *Squalidy*. His work has appeared in *Gigantic Sequens*, *Hobart*, *SmokeLong Quarterly*, and *yemassee*, among others. He is working towards his MFA in fiction at Minnesota State University.

JUNED SUBHAN is a writer from England whose work has been published in many literary journals including, recently, *Ontario Review*. He is currently working on a novel.

ELIZABETH TANNEN worked as an editor and producer of NPR's *All Things Considered* from 2005-8. Her essays, stories, and poems appear in *Front Porch*, *The Rumpus*, *Salon*, *Southern Humanities Review*, and elsewhere. She lives in Minneapolis, where she teaches and curates the monthly reading series Fiver Writers, Five Minutes, Five Watt and Five Watt Coffee.

ELLEN DORÉ WATSON's forthcoming fifth full-length collection is *pray me stay eager* (Alice James, 2018). Her work has appeared in *The American Poetry Review*, *The New Yorker*, *Orion*, and *Tin House*. She has translated a dozen books from Brazilian Portuguese, including the work of Adélia Prado. Watson edits poetry for *The Massachusetts Review*, directs the Poetry Center at Smith College, and teaches in the Drew University Low-Residency MFA program.

LESLEY WHEELER is the author of four collections, including *Radioland* (Barrow Street, 2015) and *Heterotopia* (2010), winner of the Barrow Street Press Poetry Prize. Recent poems and essays appear in *Crab Orchard Review*, *Ecotone*, and *Poetry*. Wheeler teaches at Washington and Lee University in Lexington, Virginia.

PAYAM YAZDANJOO (b. 1975) is an Iranian writer who has published two collections of short stories and a novel in Persian. He has lived in Paris since 2014. For more information, see page 103.

Required Reading

(Issue 25)

(Each issue we ask that our contributors recommend up to three recent titles. What follows is the list generated by issue 25's contributors.)

José Eduardo Agualusa, *A General Theory of Oblivion*, trans. Daniel Hahn (Talia Bloch)

Alireza Taheri Araghi, Ed., *I Am a Face Sympathizing with Your Grief: Seven Younger Iranian Poets* (Poupeh Missaghi)

Lesley Nneka Arimah, *What It Means When a Man Falls from the Sky* (Elizabeth Tannen)

Rae Armantrout, *Partly: New & Selected Poems, 2001-2015* (John Gallaher)

Elizabeth Arnold, *Skeleton Coast* (Genevieve Kaplan)

Sherman Alexie, *You Don't Have to Say You Love Me: A Memoir* (Adrian C. Louis)

Derrick Austin, *Trouble the Water* (Jessica Guzman Alderman)

Clare Beams, *We Show What We Have Learned & Other Stories* (Joanna Pearson)

Josh Bell, *Alamo Theory* (Keith Kopka)

Franco "Bifo" Berardi, *Futurability: The Age of Impotence and the Horizon of Possibility* (Robert Archambeau)

Emily Berry, *Stranger, Baby* (Shara Lessley)

Tommye Blount, *What Are We Not For* (Kimberly Kruge)

Trevino L. Brings Plenty, *Wakpá Wanáǧi* (Adrian C. Louis)

Zeke Caligiuri, *This Is Where I Am* (Elizabeth Tannen)

Leonora Carrington, *The Complete Stories of Leonora Carrington* (Ashley Keyser)

Chen Chen, *When I Grow Up I Want to Be a List of Further Possibilities* (Wendy Chen)

Garrard Conley, *Boy Erased: A Memoir of Identity, Faith, and Family* (Peter LaBerge)

Patty Yumi Cottrell, *Sorry to Disrupt the Peace* (Alex McElroy)

Tadeusz Dabrowski, *Black Square*, trans. Antonia Lloyd-Jones (Michael Bazzett)

Matthew Desmond, *Evicted: Poverty and Profit in the American City* (Juned Subhan)

Michael Dickman, *Green Migraine* (Margaret Cipriano)

Anaïs Duplan, *Take This Stallion* (Elizabeth Scanlon)

Carolina Ebeid, *You Ask Me to Talk About the Interior* (Ellen Doré Watson)

Paul Ebenkamp, *The Louder the Room the Darker the Screen* (Graham Foust)

Jenny Erpenbeck, *The End of Days*, trans. Susan Bernofsky (Viet Dinh)

Jill Alexander Essbaum, *Hausfrau* (Juned Subhan)

Kathy Fagan, *Sycamore* (John Gallaher)

Siobhan Fallon, *The Confusion of Languages* (Shara Lessley)

Alan Felsenthal, *Lowly* (Kate Berson & Velma García-Gorena)

Rita Felski, *The Limits of Critique* (Patrick Errington)

Elena Ferrante, *Neapolitan Novels*, trans. Ann Goldstein (Michael Bazzett)

Vievee Francis, *Forest Primeval* (Kimberly Kruge)

Kerri French, *Every Room in the Body* (Stephanie Rogers)

Roxane Gay, *Hunger: A Memoir of (My) Body* (Kate Berson & Velma García-Gorena)

Melody S. Gee, *The Dead in Daylight* (Wendy Chen)

Aracelis Girmay, *the black maria* (Chelsea Dingman)

Jennifer Givhan, *Protection Spell* (Kimberly Kruge)

Louise Glück, *American Originality: Essays on Poetry* (Tony Hoagland)

Melissa Goodrich, *Daughters of Monsters* (Pete Stevens)

Camilla Grudova, *The Doll's Alphabet* (Alex McElroy)

Yaa Gyasi, *Homegoing* (Meagan Ciesla)

Jonathon Haidt, *The Righteous Mind: Why Good People Are Divided by Politics and Religion* (Kyle McCord)

James Allen Hall, *I Liked You Better Before I Knew You So Well* (Jehanne Dubrow)

Mohsin Hamid, *Exit West* (Pete Stevens)

Yuval Noah Harari, *Sapiens: A Brief History of Humankind* (Talia Bloch)

francine j. harris, *play dead* (Sara Eliza Johnson)

Robert Hass, *A Little Book on Form* (Michael Bazzett)

Lily Hoang, *A Bestiary* (Joseph O. Legaspi)

Cara Hoffman, *Running: A Novel* (Joel Morris)

Jay Hopler, *The Abridged History of Rainfall* (Chelsea Dingman)

Marie Howe, *Magdalene* (Sarah Carson)

Nick Joaquin, *The Woman Who Had Two Navels and Tales of the Tropical Gothic* (Joseph O. Legaspi)

John Jodzio, *Knockout* (Pete Stevens)

Jenny Johnson, *In Full Velvet* (Dilruba Ahmed)

Patricia Spears Jones, *A Lucent Fire: New & Selected Poems* (Tony Hoagland)

Rodney Jones, *Village Prodigies* (James Dunlap)

Judy Jordan, *Carolina Ghost Woods* (James Dunlap)

Michael Kaan, *The Water Beetles* (Robert Archambeau)

Rachel Kadish, *The Weight of Ink* (Kevin Prufer)

Han Kang, *The Vegetarian*, trans. Deborah Smith (Genevieve Kaplan)

Ginger Ko, *Inherit* (Jessica Guzman Alderman)

Jean Hanff Korelitz, *The Devil and Webster* (Joel Morris)

Geeta Kothari, *I Brake for Moose & Other Stories* (Dilruba Ahmed)

László Krasznahorkai, *The Last Wolf & Herman*, trans. John Batki & George Szirtes
  (Viet Dinh)

Sueyeun Juliette Lee, *Solar Maximum* (Sara Eliza Johnson)

Dana Levin, *Banana Palace* (John Gallaher)

Jen Levitt, *The Off-Season* (David McLoghlin)

Valeria Luiselli, *Tell Me How It Ends: An Essay in 40 Questions* (Kate Berson
  & Velma García-Gorena)

Alison MacLeod, *All the Beloved Ghosts* (Joanna Pearson)

Kelly Magee, *The Neighborhood* (Kyle McCord)

Randall Mann, *Proprietary* (Jehanne Dubrow)

Maurice Manning, *One Man's Dark* (James Dunlap)

Douglas Manuel, *Testify* (Wendy Chen)

Amelia Martens, *The Spoons in the Grass Are There to Dig a Moat* (Stephanie Rogers)

Raoul Martinez, *Creating Freedom: The Lottery of Birth, the Illusion of Consent, and the
  Fight for Our Future* (Juned Subhan)

Airea D. Matthews, *Simulacra* (Robert Archambeau)

Matt Mauch, *Bird Brain* (Kyle McCord)

Shane McCrae, *In the Language of My Captor* (Shara Lessley)

Elizabeth Metzger, *The Spirit Papers* (Patrick Errington)

Jenny Molberg, *Marvels of the Invisible* (Jessica Guzman Alderman)

Matthew Olzmann, *Contradictions in the Design* (Joseph O. Legaspi)

Alicia Suskin Ostriker, *Waiting for the Light* (Cynthia Hogue)

Alan Michael Parker, *The Ladder* (Cynthia Hogue)

Rebecca Hazelton & Alan Michael Parker, Eds. *The Manifesto Project* (Kevin Prufer)

Morgan Parker, *There Are More Beautiful Things Than Beyoncé* (Sarah Carson)

Elena Passarello, *Animals Strike Curious Poses* (Andrew Cartwright, Margaret Cipriano,
  Hasanthika Sirisena)

Daniel Pennac, *Diary of a Body*, trans. Alyson Waters (Patrick Errington)

Rowan Ricardo Phillips, *Heaven* (Graham Foust)

Lia Purpura, *Rough Likeness: Essays* (Hasanthika Sirisena)

Jacques Rancourt, *Novena* (Ashley Keyser)

Iván Repila, *The Boy Who Stole Attila's Horse*, trans. Sophie Hughes (Viet Dinh)

Brynne Rebele-Henry, *Fleshgraphs* (Peter LaBerge)

Max Ritvo, *Four Reincarnations* (Peter LaBerge)

Jane Satterfield, *Apocalypse Mix* (Lesley Wheeler)

Mike Scalise, *The Brand New Catastrophe* (Andrew Cartwright, Joanna Pearson)

Samantha Schweblin, *Fever Dream*, trans. Megan McDowell (Kate Berson & Velma García-Gorena, Alex McElroy)

Natalie Shapero, *Hard Child* (Keith Kopka)

Solmaz Sharif, *Look* (Poupeh Missaghi)

Michael Shewmaker, *Penumbra* (Jehanne Dubrow)

Ed Skoog, *Run the Red Lights* (David McLoghlin)

Tracy K. Smith, *Ordinary Light: A Memoir* (Lesley Wheeler)

Dana Spiotta, *Innocents and Others* (Graham Foust)

Nicole Steinberg, *Glass Actress* (Elizabeth Scanlon)

Kanishk Tharoor, *Swimmer Among the Stars* (David McLoghlin)

Heather Tone, *Likenesses* (Elizabeth Scanlon)

Sara Uribe, *Antígona González*, trans. John Pluecker (Genevieve Kaplan)

Ocean Vuong, *Night Sky with Exit Wounds* (Talia Bloch, Ellen Doré Watson)

Afaa Michael Weaver, *Spirit Boxing* (Cynthia Hogue)

Allison Benis White, *Please bury me in this* (Chelsea Dingman)

Ross White, *The Polite Society* (Dilruba Ahmed)

Joel Whitney, *Finks: How the C.I.A. Tricked the World's Best Writers* (Poupeh Missaghi)

Jennifer Willoughby, *Beautiful Zero* (Elizabeth Tannen)

David Wojahn, *For the Scribe* (Lesley Wheeler)

Monica Youn, *Blackacre* (Sara Eliza Johnson)

Dean Young, *The Art of Recklessness: Poetry as Assertive Force and Contradiction* (Ellen Doré Watson)

Abigail Zimmer, *girls their tongues* (Sarah Carson)

The Copper Nickel Editors' Prizes
(est. 2015)

(Two $500 prizes awarded to the most exciting work published in each issue, as determined by a vote of the Copper Nickel staff)

Past Winners

spring 2017 (issue 24)

Ashley Keyser, poetry
Robert Long Foreman, prose

fall 2016 (issue 23)

Tim Carter, poetry
Evelyn Somers, prose

spring 2016 (issue 22)

Bernard Farai Matambo, poetry
Sequoia Nagamatsu, prose

fall 2015 (issue 21)

Jonathan Weinert, poetry
Tyler Mills, prose

spring 2015 (issue 20)

Michelle Oakes, poetry
Donovan Ortega, prose

Welcome to our new website:
www.laurelreview.org

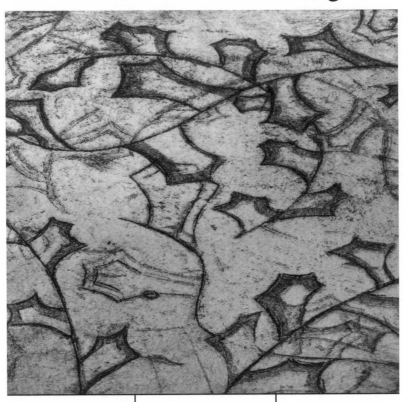

Sumbmissions	Subscribers	Issues

Inaugural winner of the Jake Adam York Prize

Analicia Sotelo's
VIRGIN

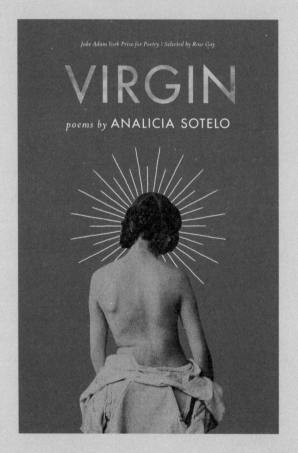

forthcoming from Milkweed Editions in February 2018

milkweed.org/author/analicia-sotelo

COPPERNICKEL

subscription rates

For regular folks:

one year (two issues)—$20
two years (four issues)—$35
three years (six issues)—$45
five years (ten issues)—$60

For student folks:

one year (two issues)—$15
two years (four issues)—$23
three years (six issues)—$32
five years (ten issues)—$50

For more information, visit: www.copper-nickel.org.

To go directly to subscriptions
visit: www.regonline.com/coppernickelsubscriptions.

To order back issues, call 303-556-4026
or email wayne.miller@ucdenver.edu.